ROCKY MOUNTAIN NATIONAL PARK

DAYHIKER'S GUIDE

A SCENIC GUIDE TO 33 FAVORITE HIKES INCLUDING LONGS PEAK

JEROME MALITZ

JOHNSON BOOKS
Boulder

Library of Congress Cataloging-in-Publication Data
    Malitz, Jerome, 1936–
      Rocky Mountain National Park dayhiker's guide: a scenic guide to 33 favorite hikes including Longs Peak / Jerome Malitz.—1st ed.
      p.   cm.
     ISBN1-55566-110-6
     1. Hiking—Rocky Mountain National Park (Colo.)—Guidebooks.
2. Rocky Mountain National Parks (Colo.)—Guidebooks. I. Title.
GV199.42.R62M35 1993
917.88'69—dc20   92-42538
                                                  CIP

Front Cover Photograph: The Loch, by Jerome Malitz
Back Cover Photograph: Trail to Finch Lake, by Jerome Malitz
Design and Typesetting: Shadow Canyon Graphics, Evergreen, Colorado
Maps: Trails Illustrated, P.O. Box 3610, Evergreen, Colorado 80439
(800) 962-1643
The maps included in this guide are from Trails Illustrated's Rocky Mountain National Park map, which is for sale at park visitor centers. It is highly recommended that the complete map be carried for all hikes in this guide. Hike numbers appear on the map denoting the destination or general area of the thirty-three hikes described in the guide.

6 7 8 9

Printed in the United States of America by
Johnson Printing Company
1880 South 57th Court
Boulder, Colorado 80301

WARNING: Hiking in mountainous terrain can be a high-risk activity. This guidebook is not a substitute for your experience and common sense. The users of this guidebook assume full responsibility for their own safety. Weather, terrain conditions, and individual abilities must be considered before undertaking any of the hikes in this guide.

Contents

Acknowledgements

My thanks to my wife Suzy, who accompanied me on nearly all of the hikes described, kindling my enthusiasm or counseling patience as the situation required. She also helped with the editing and word processing. Some of her photos appear on pages 95 and 131.

And to my longtime friend and colleague Richard Holley, who joined me on some of the longer hikes, and contributed several photographs to the project (see pages 40 and 41). Dick and his straw sombrero give scale to many of the scenes pictured.

And to the fine folks at Trails Illustrated whose map of the park is an indespensible companion in any hiker's pack.

And to the many park rangers who so patiently, unselfishly, and cheerfully shared their knowledge and experience with me.

And to those park personnel who read the manuscript and offered many invaluable suggestions and corrections.

To all these and many more, my gratitude and thanks.

Aspen midway to lake from the Bierstadt Lake trailhead

Preface

Rocky Mountain National Park is one of our greatest scenic treasures. Within its boundary are some of the most magnificent peaks, alpine lakes, and high-country valleys to be found anywhere on the continent. So it is not surprising that millions of people come to the park each year. And there is no better way to enjoy the scenery than on foot, strolling through a meadow awash with wildflowers, or walking across the sun-drenched alpine tundra, or hiking through some shady forest up to timberline and then onto some grand summit with a view over thousands of square miles.

In words and photographs, this book describes some of the best day-hikes in Rocky Mountain National Park, emphasizing not only the destination of the hike, but the remarkable features you see along the way.

Except for the hike to Longs Peak, the hikes described here require less than 4,000 feet of elevation gain and a total round-trip distance of no more than 10 miles. All climate zones and terrain types in the park can be experienced within these limits.

The book begins with a few words about the geology, flora, fauna, and history of the region. The treatment is brief, and is intended to entice the reader into further pursuing these fascinating topics — a pursuit guaranteed to increase the pleasure of visiting the park.

There is a general description of the climate and some suggestions on what to wear and what to carry. Although there are very few hazards associated with hiking these trails, some free advice is offered on how to avoid them.

The majority of the book is devoted to trail descriptions — an extended invitation to hike into some of the most magnificent terrain on the planet. We hope that the reader will accept this invitation, and will find this book helpful in deciding which trails to travel.

Happy hiking.

Dream Lake, Hallett Peak (left) and Flattop Mountain

Introduction

A grand train of national parks rides the crest of the Rockies from Canada through the United States: Jasper, Banff, Waterton, Glacier, Yellowstone, Grand Teton, and Rocky Mountain National Parks. The last is Colorado's contribution and is the focus of this guide. Rocky Mountain National Park embraces a part of the Rockies that is both magnificent and hospitable and offers an extraordinary variety of hiking trails. There are flat-land strolls across flower-studded valleys, gentle climbs to glaciers and alpine lakes, and summit assaults to challenge the most experienced mountaineer.

From valley floor to highest summit, the park encompasses a difference in elevation of 6,000 feet. Each gain of 1,000 feet brings a 3° F decrease in temperature — a climate change roughly equivalent to that experienced in traveling 600 miles northward. The park spans three climate zones: montane (7,000 to 9,500 feet), subalpine (9,500 to 11,000 feet), and alpine (above 11,000 feet). Annual precipitation varies with altitude, as the mountains trap the clouds and wring moisture from them: less than 20 inches at the lowest elevation, to well over 30 at the highest — with more on the western slope than on the eastern. The mountains tunnel wind and funnel water; they court the sun on their southwestern slopes, and offer more shade on the northeast. All of this produces a rich variety of microclimates, which fosters a wondrous diversity of plant and animal communities.

Plants and Animals

The plants range from the bizarre to the beautiful — from the primitive red algae growing on the surface of glacial ice, to the advanced but leafless coralroot orchid growing in symbiosis with the pines. Every elevation boasts its botanical gardens, and even the high tundra is carpeted with flowers during most of the summer.

Woody plants are well represented in the park. Conifers are particularly abundant, and include the stately ponderosa pine, the lodgepole pine, and the picturesque limber pine that is found in the most exposed reaches of the subalpine zone. Douglas fir is common, and the true firs are represented by the white fir and the subalpine fir — the latter's upper range defining timberline, where fierce winds and heavy snows twist and shear them into ground-hugging shrubs.

Deciduous trees and shrubs contribute their own special beauty to the park, particularly in areas below 9,500 feet. Magnificent willows and

Colorado blue columbine

Gaillardia

White marsh marigold

Parry primrose

Groundsel

Moss campion

Cow parsnip

Alpine daisy

Northern paintbrush

Horsemint

Wild rose

Scarlet paintbrush, pearly everlasting, wallflower, and others

cottonwoods impart an estatelike quality to the valleys and streamsides. Mountain ash, like its European relative that is so admired in our gardens, has clouds of white flowers in the spring, and scarlet berries and foliage in the fall. Mountain maple and red river birch augment the autumn color, while red-twigged dogwoods and several species of shrubby willows with coppery yellow twigs enliven the winter landscape.

The great color show is staged by the quaking aspen. Although a common species, aspens grow to uncommon splendor in this part of the country. Stands are Midas-touched with brilliant, shimmering golden yellow by mid-September — the color set off by the blue-green conifers in their company, the purple-gray mountains, and deep blue skies. 'High Country Gold' they call it, and gold fever draws visitors from around the world to see the spectacle.

And the fauna for the flora? Even the casual bird watcher is likely to be joyfully overwhelmed by the abundance and diversity of the park's feathered finery. From great blue heron to tiny pine siskin, from majestic golden eagle to irrepressible mountain chickadee, they animate the landscape in number and variety. Ducks of a dozen different species are common, and often bold enough to come ashore to panhandle. Clark's nutcracker, the gray jay, and the magnificent Steller's jay are even bolder and so plentiful that they can be delightfully pesky at lunchtime. Assorted sparrows, warblers, wrens, and juncos vie for attention; while daffy dippers, madcap hummers, and hard-headed hammers are a bit more reserved.

Nor is there a lack of mammals. Coyote, fox, deer, and elk are most likely to be observed near sunset in the valleys at lower altitudes. Bighorn sheep can appear at any time of the day, particularly at higher elevations. Making their home in the highest and most desolate regions are two of the parks most amusing creatures — the pika and the golden-bellied marmot. The first is an eight-inch frenetic bundle of fur with a stub of a tail, big ears, big eyes, and a bunnylike appeal. More common, or less furtive, is the marmot — two-feet long, built like a little bear, short-tailed and stub-eared. In some locations, such as the shore of Chasm Lake, the marmot is brazen enough to crash any picnic party, making a hilarious nuisance of itself.

Wherever there is a stream at lower elevations, you can find beaver dams and lodges, although the furry engineers themselves are seldom seen. And of course there are chipmunks and squirrels scurrying about, trying to mind your business more than theirs. Bears and mountain lions make their home in the park, but they are few in number and rarely seen. Few will be disappointed to learn that there are no poisonous snakes.

Geologic Origins

It is not only the plants and animals that lure visitors to the park, but also the spectacular beauty of the landscape itself, as magnificent a piece of alpine scenery as this planet has to offer. The park has been a geological laboratory since the beginning of the continent, and in the standing-up country of the Rockies, where erosion has time-sliced through cross sections of its history, geologists can read the evolution of these mountains, tracing their ancient granites back some 2 billion years ago when shallow seas covered the region.

The up-and-down battle to raise the Rockies began some 300 million years ago when forces that build mountains were first pitted against those that tear them down. The first great uplifting pushed the land some 2,000 feet above the surrounding seas. The geological evolution was accompanied by a momentous biological one — the first amphibians of the region crawled onto the land. But then the forces opposing the rise held sway — erosion reduced the mountains to hills, and the shallow seas once more encroached over much of the region.

Then, 190 million years ago, the building forces pushed the seas aside and initiated another upheaval. This time the rise of mountains was accompanied by the ascendancy of giant dinosaurs — Brontosaurus, Allosaurus, and Stegasaurus hunted and grazed in the subtropical valleys. The erosive forces countered, and again the terrain was leveled. Seas returned some 100 million years ago, imposing their hegemony over most of the land for the next 30 million years.

Another round of building and leveling began between 70 and 54 million years ago — a mountain mass rose three or four thousand feet above the plain. This time the phenomena was witnessed by new-fangled, furry creatures — the age of mammals had begun. Of course, the forces of erosion assaulted those fledgling mountains and reduced them to mere hills a couple of hundred feet high. But this time the seas did not return.

The final battles were joined some 18 million years ago, when the mysterious uplifting forces were abetted by occasional volcanic activity in the region; and 7 to 5 million years ago, when accelerated upward movement pushed the highlands even higher.

The mechanism which caused these successive upheavals is at the moment a mystery — one of the more vexing problems of contemporary geology. The Rockies are an example of a block range, a stretch of mountains bordered by a pair of parallel faults. The obvious conjecture, that during the upheavals the faults moved closer together, extruding the earth between them, is contradicted by evidence of a widening gap during these times, and no other theory presents a convincing solution to the puzzle. But the land did rise, and 5 million years ago the mass was there waiting to be abraded, cleaved, and quarried.

As rock-splitting ice, rushing water, and wind-driven sand raked and clawed at the land, another force — a most powerful force — was set in motion: the first great glaciers of the ice age formed some 2 million years ago, and these giant chisels of ice set to work sculpting mountains and carving canyons.

How do glaciers shape the terrain? Imagine a 20-mile long, 2,000-foot thick mass of ice in inexorable cold-flow moving down a mountain side. Such a mass will transport boulders the size of a house for miles; will grind rock against rock, streamlining them or abrading them to nothing; will deposit miles of rubble along their sides and leading edge; and, when they buckle upon themselves, will excavate basins out of solid stone. Through these actions, the glaciers created alpine lakes, deepened and widened valleys, laid down moraines, and quarried the sides of mountains.

The great rivers of ice came in waves — growing, flowing, usurping more and more land, until a temporary warming of the climate stopped their advance, pared their mass, and forced their retreat. Maybe there were four such waves, maybe there were more, but the greatest glaciations seem to have occurred between 2,000,000 and 600,000 years ago, and between 27,000 and 12,000 years ago.

There are still glaciers in the park — Andrews, Rowe, Sprague, Taylor, Tyndall, and others — mere suggestions of their great predecessors. These pretenders are but a few hundred years old, and all are under 250 feet thick. Still, they provide fascinating destinations for hikers, and give us some small hint of the forces their predecessors brought upon the land.

There are few places that can match Rocky Mountain National Park in its rich and varied geologic history. Almost everywhere one can see abundant evidence of the primal forces which shaped this spectacular terrain. There are several fine books on the flora, fauna, history, and geology of the park — many are available at the visitor centers and various shops in the park as well as in book stores. The bibliography lists some of these.

A Bit of History

On January 26, 1915, President Woodrow Wilson signed into law the bill that expanded the national park system to include a tenth member — Rocky Mountain National Park. So ended decades of struggle between those who wanted the region set aside in the name of conservation and public recreation, and those who wanted to keep it open to development

Nearing Beaver Meadows

Enjoying the view from an outcropping along Tundra Trail

and commercial enterprise. Presiding over the ceremony was the man many consider to be the father of the park — Enos Mills.

No one had fought so hard or so long for the creation of the park — for a decade he had been a mountain guide, writer, lecturer, and lobbyist. He had dreams of a park 1,000 square miles in extent, stretching from the Wyoming Border to Pikes Peak, but had to settle for 352.5 square miles, an area approximately a ninth the size of Yellowstone. Now that the park attracts some 3 million visitors a year, not much less than Yellowstone, the wisdom of his original plan seems more and more apparent.

Of course, the founding of the park was preceded by a lengthy history of interest and activity in the surrounding area. There is some evidence that people migrated from Alaska into this region 7,500 years ago — some say 11,000 years ago. Several Indian tribes — Ute, Shoshone, Apache, Comanche, Kiowa, Arapaho, and Cheyenne trapped and traded, hunted and made war here for at least 400 years — maybe a thousand years according to Ute legend. The Old Ute Trail that crosses Trail Ridge Road and the Continental Divide testifies to their familiarity with the area. Projectile points and other stone tools have been found throughout the park.

Indian tales tell of eagle hunts on the top of Longs Peak well before its 'discovery' by Major Stephen Long in 1820. The major was one of the leaders of the ambitious Yellowstone Expedition that was mounted to gather information and establish American hegemony in the region, and he earned his namesake mountain by never getting closer to it than 40 miles. In 1868, Major John Wesley Powell, the one-armed explorer, adventurer, and Civil War hero, led an expedition to the summit.

Less lofty goals lured others west. The California Gold Rush was under way by 1849, and a decade later the fever struck Colorado. Joel Estes was bitten early by the gold bug and tried his luck on the west coast. After some success and a bit of wandering, he and his family moved to Colorado in 1859. In 1860 he found his way to that magnificent valley we now call Estes Park where he settled, raised cattle, and did some farming and a bit of hunting. Unable to make a go of it, he sold out and left for New Mexico in 1866.

In the mid-1870's, an Englishman by the name of Windham Thomas Wyndam-Quin, Fourth Earl of Dunraven, Viscont of Mount Earl and Adare, laid claim to Estes Park and land to the north totaling 15,000 acres. His declared aim was to establish a private hunting preserve primarily to protect the habitat from those few who visited the park each season; later it was clear that he had other, more commercial, interests in mind. There was enough public resistance to his schemes and scheming ways to cause him to drop his claims.

In 1903 Freelan O. Stanley moved to Estes Park from Massachusetts, perhaps for reasons of health — the doctors had given him one year to live. But he took 37 more, and died in 1940 at the age of 91, proving again that nothing is better for health than Rocky Mountain air. This was the same Stanley who invented the Stanley Steamer and the Stanley Dry Plate for photography — a man of means, foresight, and business savvy. He bought land in Estes Park and built the grand hotel which still stands and bears his name. Unlike Lord Dunraven, Stanley had a deep interest in preserving the region for public use, an interest which he shared with his good friend Enos Mills. While Stanley locally promoted the idea of a protected region, Mills continued his campaign for a park through writings and lobbying efforts. Six years after the building of the hotel, Rocky Mountain National Park became a reality. But even these two, with all their foresight, could not have imagined how quickly the park's popularity would rise.

In 1916 there were 51,000 visitors; 1920 saw 241,000. In 1932, Trail Ridge Road opened for travel across the Continental Divide, replacing the Fall River Road which had been in place before the founding of the park. That year 292,000 visitors came in 83,000 automobiles, in spite of the Great Depression. By 1938, the number had risen to 660,000 visitors in 200,000 cars. Then came the great war, and the mid-forties saw a drop to 130,000. When hostilities and gasoline rationing ended in 1947, there were 900,000 visitors; over 1 million in 1948. By the mid-fifties, the number rose to more than 1.5 million; and by 1978, more than 3 million people a year were coming to visit the Park.

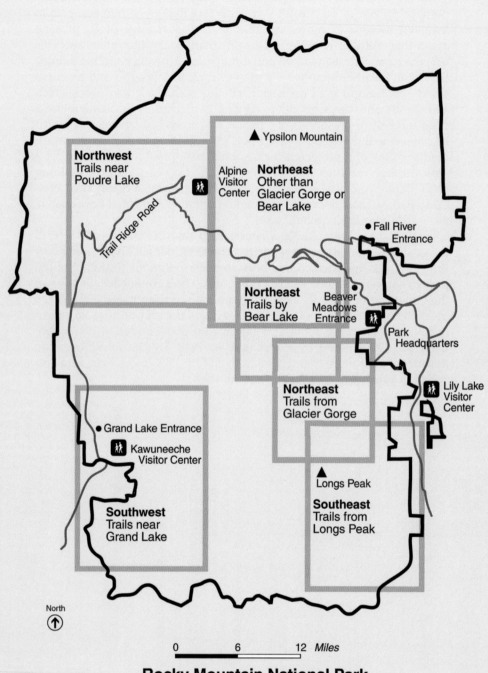

Northwest
Trails near
Poudre Lake

▲ Ypsilon Mountain

Alpine
Visitor
Center

Northeast
Other than
Glacier Gorge or
Bear Lake

Trail Ridge Road

● Fall River
Entrance

Beaver
Meadows
Entrance

Northeast
Trails by
Bear Lake

Park
Headquarters

Northeast
Trails from
Glacier Gorge

● Grand Lake Entrance

Kawuneeche
Visitor Center

Lily Lake
Visitor
Center

▲ Longs Peak

Southwest
Trails near
Grand Lake

Southeast
Trails from
Longs Peak

North
↑

0   6   12 *Miles*

Rocky Mountain National Park

Preparations

Every year thousands of people of all ages hike in Rocky Mountain National Park, but a few precautions are in order:

Weather. In Colorado's high country the rule is to expect the unexpected. It's not unusual to experience 50°s in January or a snowstorm in August. A sunny morning at Bear Lake can turn into a freezing rain atop Hallett Peak. Go prepared with clothing for all extremes and remember that weather can change rapidly with little warning.

Proper Dress. Dress in layers, prepared to peel off a layer or slip on another. Raingear is particularly essential during inevitable summer thunderstorms.

Items To Carry. Start with a day-pack with the essentials of waterproof matches, map and compass, pocket knife, space blanket or poncho, first aid kit, nylon cord, water bottle, extra food, sunglasses and sunscreen, and a flashlight. Add to the list depending on season and duration of hike.

Food and Drink. Carry high-energy food to suit your taste and plenty of water. Exertion, altitude, and wind conspire to dehydrate the body. Giardia microbes, which cause dysentary-like symptoms if ingested, require that water from streams be filtered or boiled before drinking.

Altitude Sickness. Headaches, dizziness, and light nausea may be early symptoms of altitude sickness. Visitors from lower elevations are particularly susceptible and should descend if symptoms occur.

Hypothermia. Severe chill, nausea, disorientation, and profound lethargy may be symptoms of hypothermia, which is a loss of body temperature due to factors such as improper dress, dehydration, exhaustion, exposure, and poor physical condition. Change into dry clothing, put on additional clothing, drink warm liquids, and descend to lower elevations as quickly as possible. Hypothermia can occur anytime of year.

Natural Hazards. Lightning is common during summer thunderstorms. Avoid high points and exposed areas if a storm is approaching and descend. Exercise caution around the many waterfalls and streams. Many banks and overlooks are loose and slippery, particularly when wet. Wildlife should be viewed only from a safe distance. This is their home, and here you are the guest. Winter travel has added dangers of frostbite and avalanche and should be undertaken only by those fully experienced in such matters.

Maps. The maps in this guide are from Trails Illustrated's Rocky Mountain National Park map. Hike numbers denote the destination or general area of the hikes as numbered in the guide.

Remember, this guide is not a substitute for your common sense and hiking experience. Always consider your general health and physical condition and that of your companions when selecting a trail. Then, walk softly with respect for the land around you.

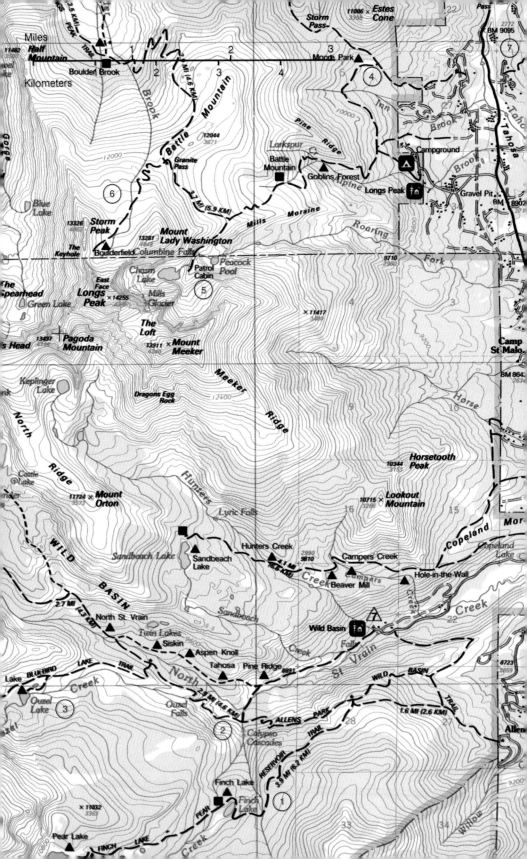

SOUTHEAST
Trails Near Longs Peak

1 — Finch Lake

2 — Calypso Cascades and Ouzel Falls

3 — Ouzel Lake

4 — Estes Cone

5 — Chasm Lake

6 — Longs Peak

7 — Twin Sisters Mountain

If you're looking for landscapes rich in water features, you cannot do better than hike in the Wild Basin area of the southeast region. Here there are tranquil lakes, superb river scenery, cascades and waterfalls. On the other hand, only a few miles away, are two hikes to mountain summits. One offers fine views of Longs Peak along the way and a panoramic view from the top; while the other is the most famous hike in the park — the climb to the summit of Longs Peak.

These trails can be reached by traveling south on Colorado 7 from Estes Park; alternatively, pick up Colorado 7 heading west out of Lyons to the southeast corner of the park where the road turns north. Driving the entire section of this highway along the eastern boundary of the park is a treat — the scenery is spectacular.

Finch Lake

Trailhead (1):	0.2 miles east of the Wild Basin Ranger Station
Distance one way:	4.5 miles
Altitude gain:	1,440 feet
Elevation at destination:	9,910 feet

The hike to Finch Lake takes you through a variety of pleasant and interesting landscapes — forests of mixed conifers, superb aspen glens, and a soberly fascinating area devastated by fire. The lake itself, nestled among trees and displayed against the massive form of Copeland Mountain, is a study in tranquility.

There is a web of routes that lead into the Finch Lake Trail, but the most direct begins at the appropriately named Finch Lake Trailhead, located about 0.2 miles east of the Wild Basin Ranger Station.

The first mile of trail ascends somewhat steeply through dense forest of pine and fir — shady and moist enough to nurture sizable patches of moss, studded here and there with parsley ferns. During late summer it's slow going along this stretch since wild raspberries are ripening within an arm's reach of the path. Redberry elder is also ripening its fruit, but for decoration only — these berries are toxic. By mid-September, the grouseberry shrublets that cover so much of the forest floor take on tints of yellow, rose, and coppery red. But the black berries that this blueberry relative produces are seldom a temptation, thanks to the abundance of grouse in the area.

The trail hooks to the right (southwest), and the second mile is signaled by a leveling of the grade. The coniferous forest gives way to an open stand of young aspen, soon interrupted by a small but superb grove of mature ponderosa pine, their red trunks and deep green needles beautifully set off against the slender white stems and silvery green leaves of their deciduous companions. Then aspen again take over, the trees now much larger, straighter, and arrayed in tighter formation — a mesh of shimmering gold in late September and reason enough to hike this trail.

Several trails converge about 1.8 miles from the trailhead, but these are well sorted out by signs — continue west. Lodgepole, spruce, and fir again dominate the forest, as the trail becomes steeper and rockier. Occasionally, there are nice views of Wild Basin, Pagoda Mountain, Chiefs Head Peak, and Mount Meeker.

Finch Lake in the rain

Another crossing of trails marks the 2.3-mile point. Signs clearly indicate direction: the trail to the left leads to Allenspark, the one to the right goes to Calypso Cascades, and the one straight ahead leads southwest to Finch Lake.

The grade moderates, and the landscape undergoes a sudden and dramatic change as the trail enters the area devastated by a forest fire in 1978. Most of the trees are still standing — charred, denuded of branches, and stripped of bark, they comprise a skeleton forest, stark but fascinating. In contrast to other sections of the burn, this part seems to be making a strong comeback, with enough sapling lodgepole to approximate the original density. An abundance of wildflowers also lightens the mood, with erigeron, aster, and pearly everlasting putting on a show from midsummer into fall. Far from somber and depressing, this is one of the most interesting and memorable parts of the trail.

The burned area continues for the better part of a mile, then it's back to living forest. The path is nearly level until 0.5 miles from the lake. Here it begins to descend, gradually at first, and then quite steeply, to the marshy shore.

Aspen about a mile along the trail

The lake appears quite suddenly, and the first view is perhaps the best, with Copeland Mountain seen as a backdrop and reflected in the water. In some places, marsh grasses grow along the shore; elsewhere, the banks are spongy with multi-colored mosses. It's a pleasant and tranquil setting, just the place for a leisurely lunch and a stroll around the lake.

Those not wanting to retrace the entire route can return to the trail junction at the east end of the burn area and come back by way of Calypso Cascades. This entails an additional downhill mile, but in return you get to enjoy some of the best river scenery in the park (see p. 23).

Calypso Cascades and Ouzel Falls

Trailhead (2):	Wild Basin Ranger Station
Distance one way:	1.8 miles (cascades), and
	2.7 miles from trailhead (falls)
Altitude gain:	700 feet (cascades), and
	950 feet (falls)
Elevation at destination:	9,200 feet (cascades), and
	9,450 feet (falls)

Waterfalls, cascades, and superb riverside scenery are among the many highlights of this hike. Adding to the interest, is a walk through part of the area that was ravaged by fire in 1978, although most of the trail passes through forest whose lush growth reflects the aboundance of moisture in the area. For those who enjoy the sight and sound of rushing water and the rich environments it fosters, this trail will be a favorite.

Ouzel Falls takes its name from a lark-sized, mousy-gray bird — the ouzel — often seen cavorting in white water. Sometimes called the dipper because of its jerky bobbing motions, this Charlie Chaplin of the water-ways often seeks shelter behind a cascade — a now-you-see-it-now-you-don't trick guaranteed to amuse and bewilder.

To reach the trailhead, exit west off of Colorado 7 about a mile north of Allenspark, and drive to the Wild Basin Ranger Station. The road is paved to Copeland Lake, then unpaved for the next 2 miles to the station.

The road passes close to Copeland Lake, and soon enters a mixed forest graced with several streams — just a hint of the scenery to come. If you can, park at the ranger station — space is limited, and the lot is often full before 9 A.M. during the weekends of summer. Parking can be had on the approach road, a second best that can add a half-mile to the hike, and not the most scenic half-mile.

The trailhead to Calypso Cascades and Ouzel Falls is close to the parking lot and opposite the station. Copeland Falls is only 0.3 miles from the trailhead, although it's worthy of a much longer hike. This is not a large feature, but it is beautiful — in its setting, in its proportion, and in the way it gives play to the water.

Curb your eagerness to reach the falls and take time to enjoy the superb river scenery in the first three-fourths of a mile — a bit of the best in the park — not as spectacular as what comes later, but special in a quieter way. To enjoy it fully, explore the side path that parallels the main trail within a few feet of the banks, occasionally vanishing onto huge slabs of granite hundreds of square yards in extent. But take care to avoid those places where signs designate revegetation areas.

Snow-melt in the high country peaks during the heat of June and early July, and brings the rivers to their fullest. But by midsummer, the flow decreases, there is less whitewater, the cascades are less boisterous, and the falls less rambunctious. But the over-all effect is at least as pleasing. Now, more of the rock wall that confines the river is visible,

Ouzel Falls

Copeland Falls

there's more balance and variety than earlier, and we can best appreciate its structure and detail.

For nearly a mile the path parallels North Saint Vrain Creek. In one section the shore is defined by an enormous slab of granite, its fissures a macrame of mosses and wildflowers. Then alder, aspen and fir make way for pine as you lose contact with the river, but within 1.5 miles you again meet up with it. Crossing a log bridge near the point where Cony Creek joins North Saint Vrain Creek, the trail continues to Calypso Cascades — less than 0.3 miles further.

Calypso Cascades

Calypso Cascades is named for the delicately beautiful calypso orchid that grows along its banks, but its action and appearance seem more appropriate to the music of that name — unpredictable, jaggedly energetic, and primitive. Unless your hike celebrates the end of a particularly wet spring, do not expect to be greeted by a torrent — this is not a large feature. Nevertheless, the theme is power and energy and it is a theme that is well churned over in these cascades.

The first view of the cascades is from an overlook a few steps to the right of the trail. A huge, split boulder perches on the other side, and water from some tributary divides and foams around it. Between boulder and cascades a small group of pines has found a precarious perch — protected, yet perpetually threatened.

Further on, the cascades come crashing down through a sluiceway of enormous boulders, and passes under the footbridge that continues the trail. Upstream, the thrashing water is split by massive, rock outcroppings, the largest supporting miniature gardens complete with trees and shrubs, and all along the banks the forest is lush and verdant, in response to the abundance of water in the area. All of which makes the change in scenery that lies ahead that much more dramatic and surprising.

Ouzel Forest Fire

Soon after leaving the cascades the trail enters the area of the Ouzel Fire of 1978. Many of the dead lodgepole still stand, their trunks black with char or stripped bare to the silvery heartwood; others lie uprooted and cracked, slowly decaying in the mountain atmosphere. It's a scene of total devastation, but rather than appearing dark or dreary, it has an austere and erie beauty.

Ouzel Falls

After more than 0.5 miles the trail leaves the burn area and climbs through switchbacks to Ouzel Falls. You first see the falls from a bridge that spans Ouzel Creek and continues the trail to Ouzel Lake. This first view is not the best — the falls being a few hundred feet away and facing to the side. But it's easy to get a close-in head-on view by scrambling up to it on the left bank over boulders and through thickets — some care is needed since the rocks may be wet and slippery. A grassy bank faces the falls and on a windy day will give you a face full of spray, but climbing a nearby boulder provides a drier perch and offers the most dramatic view. It's a great place for lunch and a bit of rest before returning to the ranger station or heading on to Ouzel Lake (see p. 28).

Winter Trail

The winter route to the falls is much longer than the summer route. It begins at the ranger station, but not the Wild Basin Ranger Station within a few hundred feet of trailhead. Instead, it's the winter station, 3 miles back down the road — the summer station is sometimes open for use as a warming hut.

From the winter station the ski trail follows the road to the summer station, the initial section passing near the south shore of Copeland Lake. Here, for about a quarter of a mile, the trail may be free of snow, but the remainder of the trail is usually well packed. The skiing is easy and imperceptibly uphill along the 3 miles to the warming hut, the trail winding through forests of aspen, pine, and spruce. A fast and easy third of a mile brings you to Copeland Falls, its beauty completely hidden by snow-covered ice.

Although the river and the magnificent rocky banks are also hidden by snow, the next half mile offers some superb scenery to the right of the trail where silvery green tracery of willow, alder, and elder are delineated against the gray-black granite outcropings. Then the trail becomes steeper, and the skiing becomes more of a challenge. Cony Creek and the North Saint Vrain are all but invisible — even Calypso Cascades is covered and stilled, and Ouzel Falls, completely robed in snow, seems to have its back turned to the skier.

The ski back from Ouzel to Copeland Falls offers several challenging runs, but the last 3.5 mi. is easy enough for any beginner.

North Saint Vrain Creek

Ouzel Lake

Trailhead (2):	Wild Basin Ranger Station
Distance one way:	4.9 miles
Altitude gain:	1,510 feet
Elevation at destination:	10,010 feet

The trail to Ouzel Lake is a continuation of that to Ouzel Falls, so you get to see Copeland Falls, Calypso Cascades, and Ouzel Falls along the way. The additional 2.2 miles offer sweeping views of Wild Basin and the surrounding mountains, as well as the area devastated by the Ouzel Fire of 1978. The hike ends at a pleasant lake surrounded by forest and set against Copeland Mountain.

After leaving Ouzel Falls the trail runs along a massive rock escarpment vividly colored in red and tan, complemented by orange lichens and green mosses. Wide bands of black char still bear witness to the forest fire of 1978. But young fir trees have taken root at the foot of the wall, and arch away from it as they grow toward the light. As the trail ascends,

Ouzel Lake

Part of the Ouzel Fire burn of 1978

the landscape becomes more open, and one begins to more fully appreciate the extent of the destruction. Less than a half-mile from the falls, the trail splits. The right hand branch goes to Thunder Lake; the left, which is the one to follow, goes to Ouzel Lake, and then farther to Bluebird Lake.

Past the junction, the trail continues through the burned area. Here one looks out at miles of devastation — a cauterized landscape. Skeleton trees, reddened or charred black, some still standing, give testimony to the conflagration. Young pines, 2 to 3 feet tall, separated from each other by hundreds of feet, stand among the remains of lodgepoles that enjoyed each other's company at a distance of 6 to 10 feet. Yet, this place has a stark and somber beauty — the gray and black hues of the standing dead wood and the greens and reds of ground-covering grouseberry set against the mountain backdrop.

Within a mile of the lake you leave the burned area for the company of living trees — the change is sudden and dramatic. A few hundred yards from Ouzel Lake, a side trail branches off the main trail to the left (southwest), and follows along Ouzel Creek to the north shore of the lake. Most of the shore is well forested, but there are plenty of places near the outlet of Ouzel Creek where you can sit and relax against a tree and enjoy the scenery. The dominant peak is Copeland Mountain to the south, while Mahana Peak to the west, and Tanima Peak to the northwest complete the backround.

Those who want a longer hike can go back to the main trail and continue west to Bluebird Lake, a mile farther and 970 feet higher. But many will want to stay longer at Ouzel Lake before returning for a second look at Ouzel Falls and Calypso Cascades.

Sapling fir and red cliff

Estes Cone

Trailhead (3):	Longs Peak Ranger Station
Distance one way:	3.3 miles
Altitude gain:	1,606 feet
Elevation at destination:	11,006 feet

Estes Cone has one of the most striking profiles in the park — a perfectly cone-shaped peak, except for the fortresslike outcropping of stone that forms its summit. As its location suggests, its summit provides excellent views of Mount Meeker, Longs Peak, Twin Sisters Peaks, Estes Park, and the Mummy Range. Remains of the Eugenia Mine add historic interest, and the climb out of the forest and onto the summit is strenuous enough to add zest to the ascent.

The trail begins at the Longs Peak Ranger Station, which is reached by heading west off of Colorado 7, about 5 miles north of Allens Park. Some of the most popular hikes in the park begin here, and parking space is limited, so it usually pays to arrive early.

Starting at the ranger station, the trail to Estes Cone coincides with that to Longs Peak and Chasm Lake for about one-third of a mile, then branches off to the right (east). There are a few small stands of aspen, but most of the trail is through coniferous forest — lodgepole, pine, spruce, and fir predominate.

At the 1.4-mile mark, a bridge constructed of halved tree trunks takes you across Inn Brook to the remains of a log cabin that housed the miners who worked the Eugenia Mine, an enterprize begun and abandoned near the turn of the century, leaving no one the richer. A few hundred feet to the northwest, a mound of mine tailings abuts the shore of the stream, and a bit farther on, a rusting iron boiler stands sentry over the rubble.

The trail continues, sometimes moderately ascending, sometimes, moderately descending. There are enough descending sections to make the net altitude gain of 1,606 feet from trailhead to summit a misleading indication of the effort involved.

At the 2.5 mile mark the trail splits — the left branch heads northeast to Glacier Basin, and the right branch heads southeast up to Estes Cone. And up it is, for in the next half-mile the trail climbs 750 feet, with the last 30 feet a rock scramble closer to perpendicular than to horizontal.

Near the beginning of this last half-mile, the trail passes through an unusual, but beautiful, forest of lodgepole pine. The trees are quite

Estes Cone

widely spaced, often many trunked, old and massive — not at all like the densely packed, straight trunked stands these trees usually form. The ground is covered by gravel and sand, colored a mauve-tan except for olive green, amoeba shaped patterns of decomposing pine needles surrounding the base of each tree.

As you ascend, the trail gets steeper and more indistinct, although small cairns clearly mark the way. Here there are several sections of the trail where the forest opens to reveal superb views of Mount Meeker and Longs Peak. Finally, you arrive at a massive outcropping of rock, colorfully embellished with lichen. But this is not the summit — the trail continues a few hundred feet to a much more massive wall. Follow the cairns, and take care as you scramble up the narrow trail. This is the steepest part of the hike, but it's only 30 feet in extent, and the exposure is nominal. Nevertheless, this section of the trail warrants caution, particularly when wet.

Nearing the summit of Estes Cone

At the end of this part of the climb, you find yourself on a small plateau. But this is not the summit either. A promontory of rock rises some 15 feet above the plateau, and its the top of this that defines the true summit. Cairns start you out in the general direction, but the final few steps will be of your choosing. At the top space is limited, and it can be crowded since people tend to linger awhile — no wonder, considering the spectacular views. To the east rise the twin domes of Twin Sisters Peaks; to the southwest Mount Meeker and Longs Peak dominate the horizon; and Estes Park stretches to the northeast, at the foot of the Mummy Range. Estes Lake is a dominant feature, and closer is Lily Lake. All this for a mere three-mile hike, although the steepness of the last half-mile will be remembered.

The descent of the steep section requires at least as much care as the ascent, but then the remainder of the hike back to the ranger station is easy enough to permit full enjoyment of the forest scenery.

Chasm Lake

Trailhead (3):	Longs Peak Ranger Station
Distance one way:	4.2 miles
Altitude gain:	2,360 feet
Elevation at destination:	11,760 feet

This lake, magnificent and aloof in its stark desolation, set against the famed east face of Longs Peak, embodies the most rugged aspect of the alpine region. Before you reach the lake, you pass through three climate zones across a wonderful diversity of terrain from gentle to harsh, making this one of the most popular hikes in the park.

Starting at the Longs Peak Ranger Station, the trail ascends at a moderate incline for the first 2 miles through coniferous forest — homogeneous, except for pleasant Alpine Brook, which you cross near the 1.5-mile mark. Then, nearing timberline, the landscape opens up, revealing a sweeping view of the Roaring Fork drainage.

Three miles from the start the trail splits — the right-hand branch leads to the Boulder Field and Longs Peak by way of the Keyhole, while the left goes to Chasm Lake. The trail continues its moderate ascent across the tundra, almost always in view of Longs Peak. One of the most conspicuous and often welcome features is an outhouse dominating a rise with a commanding view of the valley below.

Continuing along the trail we get our first glimpse of Peacock Pool, 500 feet below. Although modest in size, its sparkle and color dramatically set it off from the stark surroundings — and given its blue-green shimmer, the analogy with a peacock's plumage is well-taken. Further along, you see Columbine Falls, a delicate macrame of rivulets braiding and unbraiding over the rocks from trail height to Peacock Pool, 150 feet below.

The next section of trail provides a surprising contrast to what lies behind and ahead as it continues through a marshy alpine meadow, hopscotching a stream whose former meanders define a chain of small reflecting pools. Both the stream and the pools are bordered with hummocks of grasses and sedges; Arctic willows enjoy the moisture as do all sorts of flowering plants, like the exquisite alpine gentian with its sessile, trumpet-shaped blooms of jade-like greenish white.

Scree and rock then reclaim the terrain, and the last part of the hike is a steep but short scramble up to the rim of Chasm Lake. You don't see it until you reach the ledges above the water — and then what greets you is a monumental scene of unforgettable grandeur.

Chasm Lake

Flag trees near timberline

The lake is steely-gray. No plants moderate the raw angularity of the rock that rises precipitously to form its basin. Brooding over the opposite shore, looming a half-mile above the lake, is the east face of Longs Peak, Mills Glacier at its base.

The perfectly vertical portion of the east face is the Diamond — a mecca for world-class climbers. On almost any weekend in July and August one can watch them perform — it's a slow-motion ballet on a vertical stage. But even a front-row seat is too far back for a good view, and binoculars come in handy.

There are other diversions closer at hand. Sooner or later a welcoming committee of yellow-bellied marmots will drop by to greet you. Fat as October bears, but boldly feigning starvation, they brazenly beg a hand-out — for their health, resist the cute antics, and don't give in. The much smaller but equally cartoony pika tends to ignore the intruders, while going about its business of harvesting thatch with great purpose.

Between the animals, the climbers, and the incomparable scenery, Chasm Lake is hard to leave. Although not all of the lakeshore is accessible, you can explore the eastern edge — there are many excellent viewpoints, some at the lakeshore, and others on ledges well above the water. The only thing likely to cut your visit short is one of those frequent thunderstorms that come by to badger Longs Peak in the afternoons.

Peacock Pool

Longs Peak

Trailhead (3):	Longs Peak Ranger Station
Distance one way:	8 miles
Altitude gain:	4,855 feet
Elevation at destination:	14,255 feet

The climb to the summit of Longs Peak is the only hike covered here that requires more than 10 miles for the round trip and an elevation gain of more than 4,000 feet — but the fame and popularity of the hike justifies the exception.

What makes this peak such a popular destination? Longs is the most prominent feature in the park — a 14,255-foot presence conspicuous throughout the high country. To look down on it all from its summit has been a dream of millions of visitors — 10,000 try it every year; about 3,000 succeed. The hike passes through three zones — montane, sub-alpine, and alpine — over terrain of great beauty and interest. The mountain's form is unique and imposing. Capped by a monstrous block of granite whose east face towers nearly 2,500 feet above Chasm Lake, it creates and dominates an unforgettable landscape. Add to this the mystique of history and Indian legend, and the fact that this is the only "fourteener" in the park, and the attraction is easy to understand.

The distance and altitude gain involved dictate a bit of forethought and special precautions. Since the mountain attracts afternoon thunderstorms like a magnet, hikers are advised to be off the summit by noon. This leads to two alternative strategies — start the hike at about 3 or 4 in the morning, or camp out the night before. The first is better described as a nighthike, not a dayhike, robbing those without owl vision of a great deal of the scenic pleasure, at least on the way up. The second option involves a two-day hike, and requires some advanced planning to assure a strategic campsite.

The Boulder Field, 5.9 miles from trailhead, is the most frequently used base camp, although the Battle Mountain campground is also popular. The Boulder Field is about 2 miles from the summit, is mostly free of mosquitos, and offers super views of the East Face and the Keyhole. Each campsite is defined by a waist-high, circular wall of stone — craters in a lunar landscape. Fresh water is available at several springs in the area, but possible contamination by humans, horses, and giardia advises treating the water before use, preferably by boiling. A solar outhouse completes the accommodations.

Longs Peak from the Boulder Field

Camping at the Boulder Field is by reservation only, and since there are only 8 sites, reservations are often made months in advance. Reservations can be made in person all year at the Back Country Office east of the park headquarters near the Beaver Meadows Entrance, or at the Kawuneeche Visitor Center on the west side of the park. When open for the season, reservations can be made in person at the Longs Peak Ranger Station or the Wild Basin Ranger Station. Before June 1, reservations can be made by phone by calling 303-586-4459. Cancellations can be made by phone, and doing so early allows others to use the site. Reservations for campsites on Battle Mountain are handled similarly.

The hike described here starts at the Longs Peak Ranger Station. The first two miles of trail lead through forest of pine, fir, and spruce, occasionally passing alongside Alpine Brook. The most dramatic view appears about 1.5 mi. from trailhead as the brook cascades below a wooden bridge through banks of yellow-flowered mimulus — it's tempting to linger, but there's a lot of ground to cover. Beyond the brook, subalpine fir gets the better of pine, and soon the forest shrinks to Krummholz, the elfin groves permitting expansive views of the twin peaks of Twin Sisters and the valley below.

Above timberline, at the 2.5 mile mark, the trail veers left onto pure tundra. Half a mile further the trail splits: straight ahead leads to Chasm Lake; left leads to a skyline toilet; heading right (west) takes you to Longs by way of Granite Pass.

Finally, after a couple more cobbly miles, you're at the Boulder Field with its grand view of the East Face and the Keyhole. Those spending the night here might enjoy scrambling up the ridge of rocky rubble to the south of the trail. The reward is a spectacular, straight-down view of Chasm Lake, and an unbeatable view of The Diamond, that precipitous upper portion of the East Face that has challenged the best rock climbers for decades. The ridge melds into the edge of the East Face where the old cable route took hikers to the peak. Considered a defacement, the cables were removed in 1973, and this route is now rated as a technical climb.

With the summit of Longs as the destination, the next stop is the Keyhole, a notch in the stone flange joining Storm Peak and Longs, about 0.5 miles from the Boulder Field and 500 feet above it. Framed against the sky like the claws of a crab posturing defiance, it's one of the most extraordinary features in this extraordinary landscape. The jumble of boulders that define the Boulder Field sweep upward to the Keyhole, moderately at first, and then quite steeply. To the left of the Keyhole stands a stone hut erected to the memory of Agnes Vaille. Having accomplished the first winter ascent of the East Face on January 12, 1925, she was caught in a storm and died of exposure; a companion lost fingers, toes, and part of a foot; and a would-be rescuer also froze to death.

But step through the Keyhole and these dark reflections vanish — only Alice through the Looking Glass could have experienced greater exhilaration. Glacier Gorge stretches thousands of feet below, backed

The Keyhole at sunrise

by a gathering of "thirteeners" — from left to right (southeast to north-west) Pagoda, Chiefs Head, and McHenry peaks. Often there are hawks gliding on the air currents a thousand feet below. But there is still a 1.5-mile trek to the summit, and 1,000 feet of elevation gain yet to go.

Past the Keyhole the trail begins a traverse about a third of a mile long. Here the grade is moderately downhill, although there is nearly as much exposure as in later sections. At this point, those having a fear of heights or feeling the effects of the altitude should consider turning back.

The traverse leads into The Trough where exposure is not a concern. Much of the remaining altitude gain is accounted for here, climbing over chunks of granite at an angle approaching 35 degrees. Watch out for

The Narrows (photo by Dick Holley)

Chasm Lake and Peacock Pool from the summit of Longs Peak (photo by Dick Holley)

Longs Peak from Bear Lake

falling rocks, and take care not to free any. After 0.5 miles you enter the Narrows, and exposure is again a consideration. For the most part the route is level and as wide as a generous sidewalk, but there is a short stretch where it's pinched to a couple of feet and the wall rising above takes a disconcerting tilt over the dropoff — but a few steps and you are past it.

The Narrows continues for several hundred feet to the base of Home Stretch, wide slabs of stone, inclined nearly 45 degrees, that lead to the summit 450 feet above. Although you can stand here and there, ascending or descending Home Stretch is usually done on all fours, primordial fashion, a bit inelegant, but safe. When wet, the stone is slippery, and even more caution is warranted.

Then you're on the top of Longs Peak. Hallelujah! — it's the top of the world! — well, at least locally, it's the top of the world.

The summit is as large as a football field, and nearly as flat. Every direction has its grand views. Storm Peak is to the northwest; Mount Meeker to the southeast. To the west are the mountains of the Continental Divide; to the south is Wild Basin. And 2,500 feet below the East Face is Chasm Lake and Peacock Pool.

Although the hike to Longs Peak is justifiably famous and popular, it should not be undertaken lightly. The distance, altitude, and exposure combine to make this a very strenuous one-day trip. Those who do make the climb will remember it forever.

Twin Sisters Peaks

Trailhead (4):	Twin Sisters Trailhead
Distance one way:	3.7 miles
Altitude gain:	2,340 feet
Elevation at destination:	11,430 feet

The trail to the twin summits of Twin Sisters Peaks offers some of the finest views of their big brother to the west — Longs Peak. A morning start shows the peak's east face in full light — now framed by aspen, then conifers, and finally by outcroppings of rock from the top of Twin Sisters. But there is much more to this hike than great views of Longs Peak. The trail starts in the montane zone and takes you close to the alpine zone, from dense forest to spare tundra, across a variety of landscapes.

Teepee poles and aspen in the Butterfly Burn of 1929

Longs Peak from the Twin Sisters Trail

The trailhead is reached by a short and rutty dirt road that exits east off Colorado 7 less than 1 mile north of the exit to the Longs Peak Ranger Station. The skimpy parking lot holds about a dozen cars, so it usually pays to get there early. The access road, parking lot, and trailhead are on private land. The trail itself zigzags between private and park territory with the summits on the very boundary of the two — a strange state of affairs that sees the two domains delineated here and there by barbed-wire for the first quarter of a mile. Of course, the public use of private land is a privilege which should not be abused.

The trail begins in a dense and shady forest of pine, spruce and fir, skirts a superb stand of aspen, and then snakes up the mountain through a series of switchbacks. Occasional clearings through the trees offer superbly framed views of Longs Peak. The path is within the comfortable cover of coniferous forest until the last 0.75 mi. Near timberline there are some extraordinary limber pines, thick-trunked and wind-stretched to horizontal — they seem to be levitating, taunting gravity.

The contrast between forest and tundra is sudden and spectacular, and here the trail begins to ascend through several short but steep switchbacks to the south peak of Twin Sisters. The small, cobblestone building and a radio antenna near the summit are used for park communications; the building is kept locked, and is not intended to be used as a shelter. The trail continues counterclockwise around the side of the cabin and climbs steeply up a rock promontory that caps the summit.

From here the views are spectacular: Longs Peak with companions Mount Meeker and Mount Lady Washington to the southwest; Estes Park with its divided lake to the east; the twin's other peak to the north; and the plains stretching to Boulder and Denver to the southeast. In good weather few people are quick to leave the summit, so expect some company. It's a great place to linger over lunch, take in the view, and watch the ravens perform aerial acrobatics above the peaks and in the valleys below.

Radio antenna near the summit of Twin Sisters Mountain

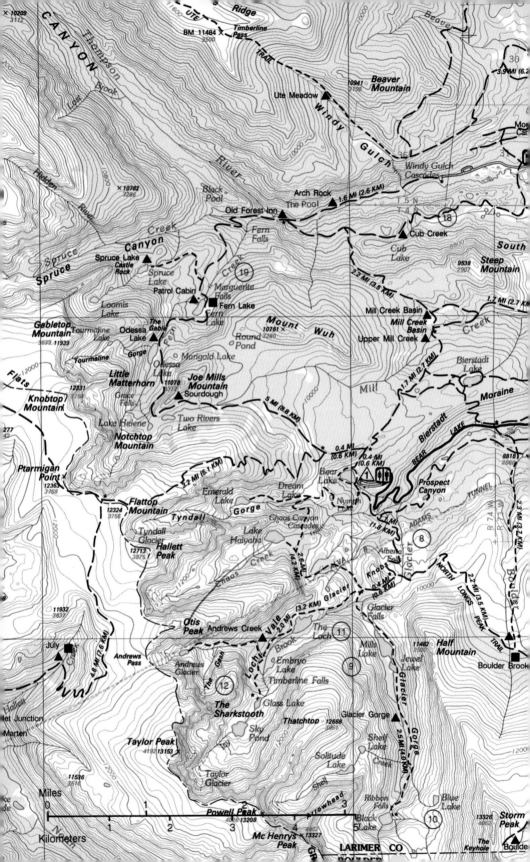

NORTHEAST
Trails From
Glacier Gorge Junction

8 — **Alberta Falls**

9 — **Mills Lake**

10 — **Black Lake**

11 — **The Loch**

12 — **Timberline Falls, Lake of Glass, Sky Pond**

The trails from Glacier Gorge Junction lead to some of the most famous lakes in the park — alpine lakes and subalpine lakes of unsurpassed beauty. Superb river scenery, cascades, and waterfalls are prominent features of these hikes, and Glacier Gorge itself is an attraction.

To reach Glacier Gorge Junction, head south from the Beaver Meadows entrance on Bear Lake Road for about 9 miles. The popularity of this region is not reflected in the size of the parking lot, and the lot is often filled by 9 a.m. on summer weekends. If space is unavailable, you can continue 0.7 miles further and park at the Bear Lake lot — a 0.4 mile trail connects the two lots. But if both are filled, which is often the case, you can return to the Bear Lake shuttle bus depot, 4.8 miles from the Beaver Meadows entrance. Here you can park your car, and take the bus to Glacier Gorge Junction.

Alberta Falls

Trailhead (1):	Glacier Gorge Junction
Distance one way:	0.6 miles
Altitude gain:	160 feet
Elevation at destination:	9,400 feet

The walk from Glacier Gorge Junction to Alberta Falls may be the most popular in the park — in part because the trail is short and easy — but mainly because it's beautiful and varied. Alberta Falls is one of the most impressive falls in the park, and along the trail you see scenic Glacier Creek and walk along the rim of Glacier Gorge.

Early on, the trail passes through several superb aspen groves, but almost all the trees within 10 feet of the trail have paid for their beauty with their hides — an anthology of travel and infatuation carved into

Glacier Gorge

the bark. It's difficult to understand why people drawn to visit the park are driven to such thoughtless and irresponsible vandalism. Still, the landscape is magnificent — marred, but magnificent.

About halfway to the falls the path angles to the right onto a balcony of rock that falls away in a nearly vertical drop to the river below — one of the most spectacular overlooks of Glacier Gorge.

Glacier Creek meanders beside the trail; sometimes you hear only its music, other times you see it through the aspens. There are places where the trail comes within 20 feet of the bank, and one can easily descend to the water's edge to view some of the best streamside scenery in the

Alberta Falls

park. Aspen, alder, willow, redberried elder, red-ozier dogwood, and fir populate the banks; Parry primrose, monkey flower, blue chiming bells, cowparsnip, monarda, lady's tresses, and dozens of other wild flowers add sparks of color during much of the summer.

Alberta Falls itself comes thundering into view quite suddenly, careening against the walls of the granite chute it carved for itself. The passage, too stingy in width for the amount of water transported, constricts the river to foam as it tumbles down the narrow canyon. The banks and surrounding terrain consist of large slabs of granite and huge boulders. Snaky aspen emerge from the crevices in the rock and between the boulders, seeming to survive without the benefit of soil. This remarkable grove of trees, so accessible and so conspicuous, has also been totally defaced from ground level to as high as one can reach with a jackknife. The rock ledges that define the canyon are easily climbed, and offer spectacular views of the river as it hurls itself into the descent.

After a stop at the falls many turn back, but the path continues on to some of the most renowned lakes in the park: Mills, Haiyaha, and The Loch. This is another reason why the trail is so popular.

Winter Trail to Alberta Falls

In winter, the trail from the Glacier Gorge parking lot to Alberta Falls is a beginner's ski or easy snowshoe trek, with the steepest ascent beginning and ending within a few hundred yards of the trailhead. At this time of year, the creek paralleling the trail is encased in ice and covered by snow, concealing one of the trail's most pleasant summer features. But winter offers its own special treats. Here and there groups of young, pale gray-green aspen stand alone or are interwoven with an occasional fir or pine. Near the halfway mark, where the trail bends sharply to the right, the hiker is brought to the rim of Glacier Gorge, even more imposing in winter than at other seasons. The wall facing you is clear of snow except for the rim and a delicate tracing woven into the crevices of the nearly vertical sides.

In deep winter, Alberta Falls is hidden by a blanket of snow, and there is no indication of its roller-coaster rush through the rock chute to the boulders below. The trail past the falls continues up to Mills Lake, The Loch, and Haiyaha, but is seldom followed in winter since there are stretches that are regularly raked by high winds, and others that pose an avalanche hazard. Fortunately, there are safer alternate routes that get you to the first two during winter (see p. 54).

Mills Lake

Trailhead (1):	Glacier Gorge Junction
Distance one way:	2.5 miles
Altitude gain:	700 feet
Elevation at destination:	9,950 feet

Enos Mills was one of the park's great heroes. From 1884 to 1922, he made his home in these mountains, acting as a naturalist and guide, popularizing the area through his writings, and tirelessly campaigning for the establishment of a national park. Mills Lake is named in his honor, and what a memorial it is. No lake is more beautiful or has a more impressive backdrop. The hike passes through such superb scenery that most would consider it reward enough, even without the incomparable lake at its destination.

Mills Lake

Dwarfed fir backed by the Keyboard Of The Winds

The initial part of the trail is the route from Glacier Gorge Junction to Alberta Falls (see p. 48) — a treat in itself, but there is so much more to come. Soon after leaving the falls, the trail climbs moderately along a hillside above Glacier Brook, then snakes upward more steeply to the junction of trails leading to Loch Vale, Haiyaha, and Mills. Here you take the branch to the left (south). The path soon crosses a bridge at Icy Brook about a half-mile from the lake, and the ascent becomes steeper. Several switchbacks lead from spruce and fir forest onto enormous slabs of granite, their fissures and abutments hoarding enough soil to nurture dwarf gardens of subalpine fir, limber pine, ground-hugging juniper, yellow-flowering potentilla, and an assortment of hummocky alpine plants studded with bloom throughout most of the summer.

The trail levels off at the lake's outlet to Glacier Creek, the stream drawn out from an extension of Mills Lake flowing lazily through a gorge of massive granite boulders. Here and there a rocky island rises from the water, decorated with grasses, sedges, willows and an occasional fir.

A short walk takes you to the northeast shore of Mills, and presents a landscape of such grandeur that even the magnificent scenery encountered on the approach is not likely to lessen the impact.

The lake is close to timberline — yet alpine fir, limber pine, juniper, and other conifers thrive along its shores. The trees are not large, but they are densely foliaged and grouped into tightly knit stands. Moist and dry areas are juxtaposed on the banks, so that one can find ferns and blue chimingbell within a few steps of saxafrage, erigeron, and sedum.

In some places the forest reaches to the water's edge; in others, rock ledges define the shore and intrude into the lake. It's an irresistible invitation to stay awhile and take in as much of the scene as possible.

Across the lake, the northwest shoreline is defined by massive granite blocks stacked to a sheer escarpment rising some 40 feet above the water. Towering in the background, from southeast to southwest, are the peaks of Longs, Chiefs Head, McHenrys, and Thatchtop mountains.

The Mills Lake Trail continues along the eastern shore, leaving bedrock for more boggy terrain. At the south end of Mills and contiguous with it is Jewel Lake — what division there is between the two is due to the industry of beavers. Unlike the hard-edged contours of Mills, the shores of Jewel are marshy and not clearly defined. It lacks the grandness of its companion, but the delicate grasses on its perimeter give it a gentle, impressionistic character that complements Mills hard-edged and rugged aspect.

Escarpment at the mouth of Mills Lake

Erratic at lakeside

Those who can pull themselves away from this area have several options: onward another 2.2 mi. to Black Lake (see p. 56); back to the trail junction for a hike to The Loch or Haiyaha; or simply return to Glacier Gorge Junction, maybe with a stop at Alberta Falls. Choosing the best among the best is never easy.

Mills Lake in Winter

The winter route to Mills and The Loch branches off to the right (south) from the Alberta Falls Trail at the second wooden bridge close to the starting point. A pack trail in summer, it's more direct but steeper — not difficult for the snowshoer but a challenge to the intermediate skier. It's an interesting and varied route, winding in and out of pine forests, aspen stands, between rock outcroppings, and finally to a junction of trails leading to Haiyaha, Mills, The Loch, and Alberta Falls. The orientation of the signs and their inscriptions is somewhat confusing and one should take a moment to read them all.

The path to Mills Lake and The Loch soon passes a hitching post for horses and continues to a wooden bridge where it splits — left to Mills and right to The Loch.

Past this point the path to Mills becomes steeper, but soon rewards the winter visitor with some majestic views of the surrounding mountains; while here and there, on the rocky ridges siding the trail, contorted limber pines bear witness to the altitude and wind.

Then, walking on the frozen surface of Glacier Creek, you enter a canyon reserved for the winter hiker — a canyon of stark beauty with black walls formed from precisely abutting boulders. This is one of the most impressive features of the hike. But there's more, for soon the canyon opens up onto Mills Lake itself, its frozen vastness cradled in the surrounding mountains. Here, in midwinter at nearly 10,000 feet, it can be bitterly cold, and icy winds are often tunneled through the mountain passes and accelerate across the frozen lake with numbing ferocity. At such times, few will stay long, but it's an experience that will be long-remembered.

Approaching Mills Lake over Glacier Creek on snowshoes

Black Lake

Trailhead (1):	Glacier Gorge Junction
Distance one way:	4.7 miles
Altitude gain:	1,390 feet
Elevation at destination:	10,620 feet

The hike to Black Lake is a 2-mile continuation of the trail to Mills Lake, going past Jewel Lake and then following Glacier Creek upstream, at times near enough to catch some spray, sometimes far enough to hear only the rushing water. The streamside scenery along the trail is superb, and at trail's end is that extraordinary, mountain-backed, black tarn.

Being so close to the creek and lakes, it is not surprising that the path is marshy in spots, and boardwalks have been constructed over the wettest stretches — more convenient, less obtrusive, and less damaging than a footpath worn through water-logged soil. But don't expect this area to be dreary. For as soon as the snow melts, yellow globeflower and white marsh marigold carpet the ground, and all sorts of other moisture loving plants spring up to make the place a garden.

The trail continues through forests of pine and fir, now and then crossing huge slabs of granite. Fissures in the rock nurture miniature gardens of mosses, sedges, and wildflowers; the larger cracks support entire landscapes complete with dwarfed trees and shrubs. Then the trail returns to Glacier Creek, while the forest opens for a view of Storm Peak to the east, and across the river to the west, Ribbon Falls divides and rebraids itself again and again as it makes its way down to the meadow. It would be an interesting feature to see at close range, but there is no path that I know of that leads to it, and the area is very marshy.

Beyond this point the trail becomes considerably steeper, the forest more sparse, and the trees less tall. Some of the finest river scenery on the hike is within the final 0.5 miles of the lake. Even in late June this section of trail may be under 5 feet of snow, and the lake itself is likely to be half-covered with ice. A bit of boulder-hopping will get you up-stream to the shore. Alternatively, you can cross the creek and scramble up to a rocky perch 8 feet or more above the lake. Either option offers superb views of McHenrys Peak and its black reflection in the water — just as the lake's name suggests. It's a scene of stark and desolate beauty — apt reward for a hike of nearly five miles.

Glacier Creek beyond Mills Lake

Lunch at lakeside

The Loch

Trailhead (1):	Glacier Gorge Junction
Distance one way:	2.7 miles
Altitude gain:	940 feet
Elevation at destination:	10,180 feet

The Loch is one of the most popular destinations in the park — a lake renowned for its beauty and majestic setting, and the trail to it offers a full measure of magnificent and varied scenery.

Beginning at Glacier Gorge Junction, the route is the same as that for Mills Lake until about the 2 mile mark (see p. 51), so one gets to enjoy Glacier Creek, Alberta Falls, and the Glacier Knobs along the way. In rapid succession the trail splits twice: first, a branch to the right (west) leads to Lake Haiyaha 1 mile away; then a trail branches off to the left (south) and heads for Mills Lake 0.5 miles away.

The branch to The Loch travels alongside and above Icy Brook. At the start of a sharp switchback there is an overlook which offers a view of the brook and a series of small waterfalls tumbling steeply down the

Autumn grasses at lakeside

The Loch

canyon. Looking down into this canyon in summer it is hard to imagine that in winter the frozen brook is the usual route snowshoers and skiers travel in order to reach The Loch.

The trail snakes upward through a half dozen or so moderately steep switchbacks, and soon delivers you to the northeast end of The Loch. This first view is among the finest. Framing the lake behind its far shore stands an honor guard of towering peaks: Taylor and Powell, astride the Continental Divide. Taylor Peak sports a glacier on its southeast flank, and Andrews Glacier can also be seen from some viewpoints. A rocky peninsula intrudes hundreds of feet into the lake, and is a popular place to stop for a rest and a snack. The southeast shore of the lake rises to a formidable escarpment known as The Cathedral Wall — a challenge to rock climbers who are often seen testing their skills here. The entire setting is at once serene and exciting, gentle and majestic.

Continuing along the path as it parallels the north and west shores, there are many spots where the hiker is invited to go down to the water's edge, or climb a rocky outcrop for a view. Often the surrounding peaks funnel breezes down their slopes and across the lake, animating its surface in a brilliant shimmer. Given a warm day, these breezes are welcome and refreshing, but can be more than bracing during winter.

There is more than enough here to warrant spending the entire day, but those wanting to continue can go on to Timberline Falls, Lake of Glass, and Sky Pond (see p. 61). Alternatively, going back to the trail

Winter storm at The Loch

junction gives the choice of heading up to Mills Lake or Haiyaha (see p. 51 or p. 72). But even those returning to the trailhead will have experienced some of the finest scenery in the park.

Getting There in Winter

The winter trail to The Loch shares its initial portion with the winter trail to Mills — a summer horse route that branches off to the right of the Alberta Falls Trail at the second bridge near the Glacier Gorge Trailhead and ascends, at times steeply, to a junction of trails leading to Haiyaha, Mills, and The Loch.

The path to The Loch and Mills passes a triangular hitching rail and then divides — the left-hand route going on to Mills, the right to The Loch.

Next the trail enters the streambed of Icy Brook, and the frozen stream itself becomes the path. As it ascends more and more steeply, the black walls of the canyon rise higher above it and incline more percipitously until one of the walls tilts past vertical and juts out over the trail. At the top of the ascent you leave the canyon, and find yourself at the northeast corner of the lake, Cathedral Wall on your left — an unbeatable entrance to an unbeatable setting. This spectacular approach is a special treat reserved for the winter traveler — during the other seasons, Icy Brook cascades through the canyon, appropriating the winter trail.

Timberline Falls, Lake of Glass, and Sky Pond

Trailhead (1):	Glacier Gorge Junction
Distance:	4 miles; 4.2 miles; and 4.6 miles respectively
Altitude gain:	1,420 feet; 1,580 feet; and 1,660 feet respectively
Altitude at destination:	10,660 feet; 10,820 feet; and 10,900 feet respectively

Here are three highly distinctive and scenic goals, all within 0.6 miles of each other. Each alone is worth a trip to the high country, but this hike offers all three plus a visit to Alberta Falls and The Loch. During most of the summer, Timberline Falls is a delicate macrame of streams rather than a plumeting torrent; while each of the two lakes in its own way exemplifies the fierce beauty of the alpine region.

The route begins with the hike to The Loch (see p. 58), and continues along the shore of the lake to leave it at the northwest end. The path follows Icy Brook upstream through coniferous forest, the conifers joined by willow, alder, elderberry, and river birch near the stream. Connoisseurs of streamside scenery are sure to be impressed by this section of the trail.

Less than 1 mile from The Loch the trail sends a branch off to the right, heading west to Andrews Glacier. With Sky Pond the goal, ignore the branch and continue on the main path, crossing several small streams which help to define a cool and shady nook ornamented with mosses, bog grasses, and a variety of other moisture-loving plants.

Within a half mile or so the forest thins and gives way to lush, marshy meadows. Timberline Falls is another half mile up the trail, and looking ahead you can see a bit of the falls and the mist it generates. The path becomes steeper and leaves the trees altogether, rising above the meadows onto a talus slope. Follow the red-flagged poles which mark the indistinct trail. Take care of your footing — some of the rocks are unstable and some may be wet and slippery.

Timberline Falls

Timberline Falls

The steep but short ascent up the slope delivers you to the base of Timberline Falls and, looking back, a superb view of The Loch some 270 feet below and 1.3 miles away. Timberline Falls is not particularly high or full, but it does have a delicate beauty that is in striking contrast to its stark surroundings. It's a branching fall, cascading down a black granite wall into a wide, shallow, cobble-filled catch basin, and then diffusely draining away downhill through dozens of ankle-deep rivulets. It's impossible to forego some boulder hopping in the runoff at the base of the falls, but there is still much more to see.

Lake of Glass

Lake of Glass is perched above the falls, set back a few hundred feet from the rim of the cliff. It's the runoff from the lake that feeds the falls. But how do you get up to it? The route is one of the park's better kept secrets — unmarked, inconspicuous, and at first glance unlikely. It's to the right of the falls as you face them, and close by — in fact, some of the runoff sometimes streams down the very route you ascend, making the boulders you use as stairs wet and slippery. In a few places — the

Lake of Glass

initial fifteen feet being the most challenging — the ledges are barely as wide as a boot, and the handholds are none too secure. Although the climb to the ledge takes only a few minutes, you will want to choose your steps carefully and watch your footing.

And when you reach the ledge, there's the Lake of Glass — mountain backed, and nestled in a cirque carved out of granite. The granite rises to massive outcroppings, bare in some places, but in others having enough seams and pockets of dirt to support a dwarf forest of subalpine fir, the trees barely 3 feet tall, wind-tortured and twisted to the contours of the rock. It's a spectacular scene.

As clear as the lake is, it is no more glasslike than many others; and more often than not, wind rakes its surface, substituting scintillating movement for glassy stillness. Scrambling over the ledges adjacent to the lake is fun in itself. In some places the rock rises to a 15 feet cliff — the perfect place to seek shelter from the wind, enjoy lunch, and relax.

To continue on to Sky Pond, less than 0.5 mi. away, proceed counterclockwise around Lake of Glass, following the cairns up a granite ledge and then down again to the shore of the lake. The trail hugs the shore for awhile, penetrating through a dense and tangled elfin forest of subalpine fir. Soon the path is blocked by a huge boulder. Scramble over its top and pick up the trail on the other side. Fifty feet further on you encounter what seems to be a more significant obstacle — a large rock

Unnamed waterfall near Sky Pond

outcropping with precipitous sides. However, just before reaching the rock, the trail veers sharply away from the lake for a few paces and then sharply switches back to a ledge on the side of the rock, narrowing to next to nothing for a half-dozen steps or so.

From this point to Sky Pond the hike is an easy stroll. The trail is clearly defined and well laid out with flat stepping stones — it seems more like a garden path than an above-timberline trail through a wilderness area. The route passes through an alpine meadow, almost devoid of trees, but lush in grasses, studded here and there with shrubby willows. In some places there are boulders surrounded by small reflecting ponds; extensive patches of the greenest moss grow where shaded by the stone.

A few hundred feet from the Sky Pond, you will see a small thread waterfall off the trail to the left (east). It tumbles over a ledge about 15 feet high. The falls are framed by shrubbery that sets it off from the barren flanks of Thatchtop Mountain behind it. Its delicate beauty and modest proportions seem magically out of place in this heroic landscape. During most of the day the waterfall is dramatically lit — but even in shade it's a gem.

Sky Pond

A hundred steps or so from this unnamed waterfall brings you to the shore of Sky Pond — desolate and magnificent. Powell Peak and Taylor Peak stand over the lake (the first southeast of the second), their flanks rising steeply from the water, all talus, scree, and smooth granite, leaving only the narrow approach to provide close access to the shore. Draped between the two peaks, its whiteness in high contrast to the dark stone, is Taylor Glacier. As is expected at these high alpine lakes, the wind is fierce and nearly constant; and as it tears across the water on a sunny day it agitates the surface to a glitter that confuses fire and ice. It's a scene of stark drama — the perfect climax to the hike.

The views coming down on the return trip are even more spectacular than those seen on the ascent. There are panoramic views of Lake of Glass, The Loch, and Loch Vale below; and, with the exception of the short but steep climb near Timberline Falls, the descent is easy enough to free our attention for the enjoyment of it all.

Sky Pond

NORTHEAST
Trails From Bear Lake

13 — Bear Lake, Dream Lake, Emerald Lake
14 — Lake Haiyaha
15 — Odessa Lake
16 — Hallett Peak
17 — Bierstadt Lake

If the park can be said to have a central hub, Bear Lake is it. Several of the most popular hikes begin here — hikes to mountain summits and hikes to lakes — hikes that take you to some of the finest scenery in the park. Here you will find trails that are short and easy, and trails that are long and strenuous that lead from dense forest to open tundra above treeline.

To reach the parking lot, take Bear Lake Road south from the Beaver Meadows entrance for 9 miles. If the lot is full, a likely event if you arrive midmorning on a summer weekend, park in the shuttle bus parking lot, 4.8 miles from the Beaver Meadows entrance and take the bus to Bear Lake.

Bear Lake, Dream Lake, and Emerald Lake

Trailhead (1):	Bear Lake
Distance one way:	1.1 miles to Dream Lake; 1.8 miles to Emerald Lake
Altitude gain:	430 feet to Dream Lake; 600 feet to Emerald Lake
Elevation at Destination:	9,900 feet at Dream Lake; 10,080 feet at Emerald Lake

Bear Lake, Dream Lake, and Emerald Lake are three of the most famous attractions in the park — not surprising, considering their beauty and magnificent surroundings. Although they share some of the same background features, they vary in character from lush and serene, to stark and rugged. These three lakes are connected by an easy trail that takes you through pleasant forest and along delightful streams. No wonder this hike is one of the most popular in the park.

Bear Lake

Although only a few hundred feet from its parking lot, Bear Lake is a scenic treasure. Behind its southwest shore rises the angular hulk of Hallett Peak; to the south and a bit east rises Longs Peak. No lake has a more impressive backdrop. An informative, self-guiding, 0.5-mile nature trail goes completely around the lake, and several benches and platforms invite you to linger for a longer look.

Nymph Lake

The trail to Dream and Emerald lakes leaves Bear Lake and proceeds through pine forest for 0.5 miles to Nymph Lake — a joy in its own right. In midsummer, the deep blue water is studded with yellow pond lilies. Flattop Mountain and Hallett Peak frame the lake on the approach, while a few steps later it's Longs Peak that again dominates the background.

Bear Lake

Leaving Nymph Lake, the path returns to the forest, every so often crossing some minor stream or marshy area replete with wildflowers. Near the 0.9-mile mark, at the rocky elbow of a sharp and steep switchback, there is an opportunity to step out onto the boulders alongside a small cascade of Tyndall Creek. It's a likely spot to spy American dippers (ouzels) — those dapper, gray, lark-sized birds with the comical, bobbing motions, that cavort around rushing water, often disappearing behind cascades. The trail continues through a few more switchbacks, and then there it is — Dream Lake.

Dream Lake

The lake deserves its name and its fame — it's magnificent. Hallett and Flattop peaks form the backdrop, here even more prominent and imposing than when seen from Bear Lake. The shore is varied and irregular — in some places it's knotted into rocky escarpments, in others it rises smoothly from the water to the forest's edge. At the midpoint of the north shore, a rugged peninsula juts out into the lake, its flanks ornamented by gnome-like limber pines. But those growing out of the rock on the northeast shore are the most picturesque of all — ancients of enormous girth, their roots gripping the rock like talons, they twist

Nymph Lake; Longs Peak is seen in the background to the right

and lean out over the water stretching the law of gravity to the breaking point. There is reason enough to stay here the entire day, but many go on to Lake Haiyaha (see p. 72) or to Emerald Lake.

The trail to Emerald Lake follows the north shore of Dream Lake, and then climbs steeply over rocks before leveling out. Another steep and rocky section follows, this one close to Tyndall Creek. Here the creek has cut its way through the rock. Yellow monkey flowers, sedges, and many other moisture-loving plants decorate the minicanyon, luxuriating in the spray of the small cascades. It's a place whose beauty far exceeds its size.

From here the trail leads through mixed forest where conifers and deciduous trees mingle among gigantic boulders. Then again the trail becomes rockier, and a final short but steep stretch delivers you to Emerald Lake.

Emerald Lake

From its shore the lake is usually more onyx than emerald, the steely water reflecting the black flanks of Hallett Peak and Flattop Mountain. It's a stark landscape — totally different from Bear Lake, and even more rugged than Dream Lake. The trail leads onto boulders that define the northwest shore, and you can climb higher for a better view. There are no trails around the remainder of the shore, since the mountains rise so steeply from the water, but this is what makes the scene so imposing.

Dream Lake in Winter

Even during winter the Dream Lake Trail draws more than its fair share of visitors, although during this season the section linking Dream to Emerald is not recommended since several parts pose a significant avalanche hazard.

The winter route from Dream Lake to Nymph Lake is easy but often slick with ice early in the season. Nymph Lake in winter is a featureless expanse of ice and snow, but Hallett Peak, Flattop Mountain, and Longs Peak, seen from the north and northeast shores, are even more imposing with a mantle of snow. At Nymph the winter trail diverges from that used in summer, leading clockwise around the southern shore of the lake, rather than counterclockwise. Then it climbs steeply to a ridge overlooking a canyon guarded here and there by massive outcroppings of rock, bare and black against the snow. Here, beginning skiers will find the going rough and even snowshoers will have to focus attention alternately between their footing and the magnificent scenery.

In the background, towering over the canyon and the surrounding valleys, are some of the highest peaks in the park, and in a short while, the trail affords a grand view of Longs Peak to the left (southeast). At this point you cross Tyndall Creek. Although the surface is frozen solid and covered with deep snow, the flow of water is usually audible underfoot. Then a few more steps brings you to a rise overlooking the lake and an unsurpassed landscape.

Emerald Lake below the saddle between Hallett Peak and Flattop Mountain

Lake Haiyaha

Trailhead (1):	Bear Lake
Distance one way:	2.1 miles
Altitude gain:	750 feet
Elevation at destination:	10,220 feet

Even in a region renowned for the variety and splendor of its lakes, Haiyaha stands out as something different. Its Indian name, translated 'Big Rocks', only hints at its ruggedness and individuality. In that circle of grand lakes — Bear, Nymph, Dream, Haiyaha, The Loch, and Mills — none is more imposing than Haiyaha.

The preferred route begins at Bear Lake and follows the trail to Dream Lake (see p. 68). Just before reaching Dream Lake, the trail to Lake Haiyaha branches left (south) and crosses a bridge. Then the trail leads to the east flank of Hallett Peak and begins to ascend, somewhat steeply at first. Soon, after a switchback, it levels out to a long traverse which provides superb views of Bear and Nymph lakes in the valley below, and Longs Peak to the southeast.

The trail descends gradually to a stream, crosses it by a bridge, and begins a gradual ascent through pine forest to the lake, about a quarter of a mile away.

Now nearing timberline, the landscape begins to harden. Only the trees of sterner stuff can survive the eight-month-long winter of gale winds and heavy snows. Some of the most ancient and picturesque trees in the park are found on the shores of Haiyaha. Burled and burly-boled limber pines bent nearly horizontal dig their talon-like roots into the rock crevices in search of a holdfast and nourishment. Enormous blocks of cleaved and quarried stone are scattered over the landscape like some metropolis in ruins. Several small pools, reflecting the sky and the massive boulders around them, anticipate Haiyaha. Scampering over the rocks brings you to the ledges above the lake. Hallett Peak rises up from the opposite shore to enhance the grandeur of the setting.

One can easily spend the day scampering over the rocks, exploring the shoreline and nearby pools. But those wanting to extend the hike can backtrack a quarter-mile to the trail junction, and continue on to The Loch, Mills, Alberta Falls, and then to Glacier Gorge Junction; or backtrack to Bear Lake.

Longs Peak from the Lake Haiyaha Trail

One of several pools near the shore of Lake Haiyaha

Ancient limber pine at lakeside

Haiyaha in Winter

Haiyaha in winter? — Yes, it's still there, but accessing it is a different matter. Unlike Mills Lake and The Loch, there are no recommended winter routes; indeed, there are no reliable winter routes at all. As snow is piled on snow, as temperature and pressure change the granular character and weaken the adhesion between layers, the trail presents an ever greater avalanche hazard.

Access from Dream Lake, the usual summer route, involves switchbacks and traverses on the east flank of Hallett, which manages to accrue more than its fair share of snow in spite of its steepness. Nevertheless, this is the safest route, and the safest time to travel it through snow is during late autumn or early winter, when the avalanche danger is minimal. Even then, caution is advised.

In winter Lake Haiyaha and the adjoining pools are encased in ice, and the ice is mantled with a thick blanket of snow. Although some of the lake's unique geometry is hidden, the ancient pines are still there, standing guard over the frozen landscape among the giant snow-capped boulders. Even under snow it's a dramatic scene.

Odessa Lake

Trailhead (1):	Bear Lake
	or: Fern Lake Trailhead (see p. 90)
Distance one way:	4.1 miles from Bear Lake; 4.4 miles from the Fern Lake Trailhead
Trailhead Altitude gain:	1,215 feet from Bear Lake; 1,865 feet from the Fern Lake Trailhead
Elevation at destination:	10,020 feet

Odessa Lake is another magnificent feature of the Bear Lake region, rivaling Nymph, Dream, Haiyaha, Mills, and The Loch in the majesty of its setting. Walking to the lake takes you through a variety of landscapes, from dense forest to open tundra. And since the trail is more than 4 miles long, the hike offers more solitude than many of the others in this region — an advantage for enjoying the trail's many amenities.

There are two approaches to Odessa Lake: a 4.1-mile route from Bear Lake, and a 4.5-mile route from the Fern Lake Trailhead. The longer route is also steeper — but for the extra effort you get the pleasure of seeing Fern Creek, The Pool, Fern Falls, and Fern Lake itself along the way. The Fern Lake Trailhead parking area is small — so plan to arrive early.

On the other hand, the approach to Odessa Lake from Bear Lake is far more dramatic. Moreover, the distance is shorter, and the altitude gain is only 1,200 feet — although this is a bit misleading, since you first climb to 10,675 feet before descending somewhat steeply to the lake at 10,020 feet.

The initial portion of the trail coincides with the route to Flattop Mountain and Hallett Peak (see p. 78), the branch point occurring just after a generous 0.5-mile stretch of path through a marvelous grove of aspen. Seeing this stand in fall color is guaranteed to propel you skipping and singing along the trail.

Past the aspen, the trail climbs gently through a dense and shady coniferous forest of spruce, pine, and fir. After about 2.5 miles, the forest yields to talus and tundra, and opens to extraordinary views of Flattop and Notchtop mountains. A sharp, right-hand turn (to the north) near the path's highest point yields the first view of Odessa Lake, about 0.3 miles away and hundreds of feet below in Odessa Gorge, a blue-green welcome mat at the base of the Little Matterhorn. As you descend, the forest obscures the lake, but occasionally an opening through the trees offers a tantalizing view of the water.

Odessa Lake

Aspen and Longs Peak near the start of the Odessa Lake Trail

The path down to the shore leaves the main trail a few hundred yards past the lake, descends to a bridge which crosses Fern Creek, then follows the creek back to its source. The first view of the lake from the shore is as spectacular as any other. Notchtop Mountain towers above the lake to the south; to the southwest, stands the Little Matterhorn, its broad cone shape capped by a cluster of upward-pointing pylons.

From the source of Fern Creek, a faint trail leads counterclockwise along the shore of the lake, more or less incorporating some boulders and rocky outcrops along the way. It is fairly easy to scramble up these rocks and find a cozy spot for lunch, rest, and a good view of the lake.

If you can't decide which route to take to Odessa Lake, consider a one-way tour using a two-car shuttle. Leave one car at one trailhead and drive to the other to start the hike. Of the two possibilities, leaving one car at the Fern Lake Trailhead and starting the hike at Bear Lake has several advantages: the small Fern Lake parking area is likely to be filled earlier in the day, and the Bear Lake Trailhead is 640 feet higher than the Fern Lake Trailhead. The trailhead-to-trailhead distance is 8.5 miles long, and it is hard to find a more scenic hike of that distance.

Crossing a talus slope toward Notchtop Mountain

Hallett Peak

Trailhead (1):	Bear Lake
Distance one way:	5.0 miles
Altitude gain:	3,238 feet
Elevation at destination:	12,713 feet

Hallett Peak is one of the most distinctive landmarks in the park — prominent by size, form, and location. It's the backdrop against which you first see Bear Lake and Dream Lake, and it's a notable feature of the Bierstadt Lake Trail. The hike takes you up through three climate zones, crosses over Flattop Mountain, traverses the ridge supporting Tyndall Glacier, and then ascends to the summit of Hallett Peak. If this suggests variety, you won't be disappointed. There are grand views throughout the hike, with the best view of all awaiting you at the top.

At the start of the hike, the trail leaves the north shore of Bear Lake and ascends through a boulder-strewn aspen grove. The tree trunks in this stand are particularly white, and contrast sharply against gray-black boulders. Morning light illuminates the trees, staging a showpiece in every season.

After a third of a mile, at the junction with a trail to Bierstadt Lake, the trail angles left (west) and continues its moderate climb through the aspen grove. The grove ends near the second trail junction — the route to the right (northwest) leads to Odessa Lake and Fern Lake, the one to the left (southwest) leads to the present goal, Hallett Peak by way of Flattop Mountain. The path enters coniferous forest dominated by spruce and fir. The trees are large, and the path well-shaded. Grouseberry, hollygrape, and bearberry carpet the floor. Cliff jamesia and mountain maple enjoy the areas of dappled sunlight where the forest canopy is more sparse.

A broad but shallow gorge strewn with enormous boulders appears to the right of the trail. The gorge is dry in summer but evokes images of a torrential river crashing to the valley below. The path veers away from the gorge in a switchback, and by successive switchbacks climbs steadily upward.

Quite suddenly the trail emerges at a clearing with a spectacular view — the Dream Lake overlook. Just as spectacular is the view to the west through a lattice of trees: Hallett Peak and its less imposing companion Flattop Mountain, the two spanned by the white drapery of Tyndall Glacier.

Hallett Peak from the Dream Lake overlook

The path continues on a moderate grade through coniferous forest — the trees, now primarily subalpine fir, becoming shorter and stouter. Further on, the forest breaks into disjoint stands of dwarf trees, each a Lilliputian garden barely head high. Soon the trees are only knee high, cowed by the gales to creep along the ground. Then even the firs disappear — timberline — and spectacular views of Longs, McHenrys, Powell, and Taylor peaks open up to the south.

Dense stands of shrubby willow, two feet high, appear in isolated patches. It's surprising to find willows up here away from any lake or river, but several alpine species are common in the park, and at this altitude the long winter snowfall and frequent summer rains provide water enough. Late in summer the willows color in hues of tawny russet; but they're at their best in early summer, densely decked-out in their furry, silvery catkins. Potentillas are also common at this altitude, reliably sporting their buttercup-like blossoms from late spring to early fall.

Continuing the hike, we soon reach an overlook — 1,300 feet down, nearly as a stone falls, is Emerald Lake. With its deep green color and wind-blown surface-sparkle, it looks like its namesake gem, and it's set like a gem among the surrounding dark gray mountains. Take notice of

Emerald Lake from the Flattop Mountain Trail

the cliff to the right (west) with its interesting striations and the dwarfed subalpine firs clinging to its shear face.

Nearly at the top of Flattop, flat as it is, the trail is still gently ascending. However, it is flat enough for basins of water to collect here and there, and though treeless, there are all sorts of dwarf plants carpeting the scree, a rock garden of alpine jewels: gentian, and erigeron, and saxifrage, and avens — hunkering about the boulders for warmth and protection from the wind, looking like hummocks of moss until they cover themselves with masses of bloom.

The hike continues across Flattop with many remarkable views along the way — views of lake-studded valleys and ridge after ridge of mountains. Longs Peak rises to the southeast, unmistakable with its cubical crown of granite and its north flank ornamented by an extraordinary ridge of pinnacles called The Keyboard of the Winds. Hallett Peak comes into view now, ahead and to the left (southeast), rising another 400 feet. From here it is nearly a perfect cone — black and featureless.

The Flattop plateau swings around counterclockwise to give access to Hallett Peak, and in the crook of the swing, the ice and snow mantle of Tyndall Glacier is plastered to the nearly vertical wall. Signs warn of the extreme hazard involved in too close a look.

To this point the trail is fairly smooth and sandy. But now, as you skirt the glacier and begin the final ascent to the summit of Hallett Peak,

Cairn marking the summit of Hallett Peak

the path disintegrates into a jumble of irregular chunks of sharp-edged granite boulders. Cairns mark the way, but the route is difficult to distinguish from the surrounding rubble that comprises the summit. This isn't an easy stretch, but neither is it very long — and soon you are at the top of the mountain, clearly marked by a right and proper minimountain of a cairn, about 6 feet high.

The view from the summit is superb: Tyndall Glacier and Flattop's top to the north; Grand Lake, Shadow Mountain Lake, and Lake Granby to the southwest; the many lakes and peaks to the east; and to the southeast, the towering hulk of Longs. You're surrounded on all sides by spectacular scenerey, and it takes some time to take it all in. So, find a soft rock, sit down and catch your breath, have lunch, and enjoy the view.

Most hikers plan to reach the summit of Hallett by midday, for in most seasons afternoon thunderstorms can be expected to well up no matter how cloudless the morning sky. At the very least, slick wet rocks and slippery portions of the trail will rob you of the easy and pleasant descent so well earned on the way up. Allowing three hours for the ascent should give you enough time.

For those unaccustomed to the altitude, this may not be a trivial hike; but a slow pace deserving of the scenery will minimize the difficulty while maximizing the pleasure.

Bierstadt Lake

Trailhead (2):	Bierstadt Lake Trailhead or (1): Bear Lake
Distance one way:	1.4 miles from the Bierstadt Lake Trailhead; 1.6 miles from Bear Lake
Altitude gain:	566 feet from the Bierstadt Lake Trailhead; 255 feet from Bear Lake
Elevation at destination:	9,416 feet

This is a short and easy trail to a pleasant subalpine lake. The route passes through an extraordinary stand of aspen, and offers sweeping views of the surrounding mountains.

The parking lot at the Bierstadt Lake Trailhead is directly off the road about two-thirds of the way from the Beaver Meadows entrance to Bear Lake; though small, the lot usually has some free slots except during the peak of the summer season and at the height of the aspen gold rush.

The hike begins in a dense evergreen forest, but as the trail ascends, there are fewer trees, and the landscape begins to open. Within the first

Bierstadt Lake

Hallett Peak from the Bierstadt Lake Trail

half-mile you are treated to exceptional views of Longs Peak to the south, the mountain framed between stands of aspen. The trail continues to climb through long swithbacks: the east-heading stretches present a red hillside spotted with gray sage; the west-heading stretches offer superb views of Hallett Peak, Tyndall Glacier, and Flattop Mountain.

After about a mile, the trail delivers you to a hillside of aspen, their trunks bone white and crooked, leaning out over the slope. The stand has an ethereal quality, particularly in the spring when the new crop of leaves emerges lime green and translucent, fluttering in the slightest breeze. But in the fall, when the alchemy of the first frosts cause the entire hillside to erupt in golden yellow, the trail becomes a showpiece.

Beyond this grove the path levels off and passes through sparse forest with interesting mixtures of pine, aspen, and juniper, enlivened during summer by the bright flower spires of golden banner. Then the forest becomes more homogeneous as lodgepole pine asserts dominance.

Soon you are at the lake. Conifers surround it, and the shore is marshy, its outline blurred by sedges in and out of the water. It's a gentle scene presented in soft focus. To enjoy the lake fully, explore the trail that leads around it. There is a dramatic view of Longs Peak from the north shore.

On the west side of the lake, the shore trail meets the Mill Creek Trail and a trail to Bear Lake. The latter is a slightly longer route than that described here but involves less altitude gain, and is the one preferred by many skiers.

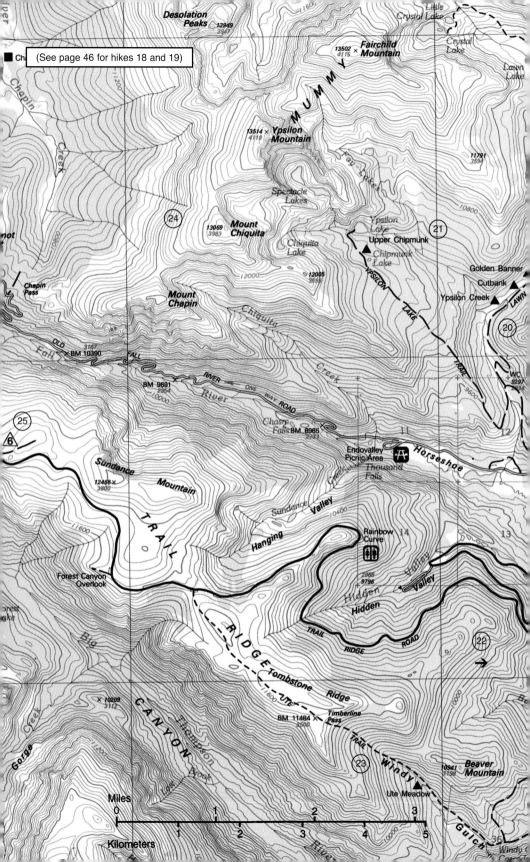

(See page 46 for hikes 18 and 19)

Desolation
Peaks
12949
3947

Little
Crystal Lake

Crystal
Lake

Lawn
Lake

Fairchild
Mountain
13502
4115

M U M M Y

Fay Lakes

Ypsilon
Mountain
13514
4119

Spectacle
Lakes

11791
3594

24

Mount
Chiquita
13069
3983

Chiquita
Lake

Ypsilon
Lake

21

10800

Upper Chipmunk

Golden Banner

Chipmunk
Lake

Cutbank

12005
3659

Ypsilon Creek

LAWN

20

Chapin
Pass

Mount
Chapin

Chiquita Creek

BM 10390
3167

OLD

FALL

FALL

YPSILON LAKE TRAIL

WC
9297

9600

RIVER

ONE WAY ROAD

BM 9691
2954

Chasm
Falls

BM 8965
9511

River

11

Horseshoe

25

6

Sundance
Mountain
12466
3800

Endovalley
Picnic Area

Thousand
Falls

Sundance Valley

Sundance Creek

10400

Rainbow
Curve

14

13

TRAIL

Hanging

2966
9796

Valley

Forest Canyon
Overlook

Hidden

Valley

Big

RIDGE

TRAIL

Hidden

RIDGE

ROAD

22

Tombstone

UTE

Ridge

10209
3112

CANYON

Thompson Brook

BM 11484
3500

Timberline
Pass

Trail

Windy

Beaver
Mountain
10941
3198

23

Ute Meadow

Gorge Creek

Miles
0   1   2   3

Kilometers
0   1   2   3   4   5

NORTHEAST
Other Than Glacier
Gorge or Bear Lake

This section of the park has a wide variety of landscapes, and the trails described here reflect that variety. One trail climbs to the summit of a mountain and offers excellent views along the way and from the top. Another is a one-way hike that starts in the alpine tundra, passes through the subalpine zone, and ends in a montane zone meadow. Another leads up through the curious rock formations of Lumpy Ridge to a lake set in a stone amphitheater. The other three trails end at mountain-backed lakes. One trail takes you along spectacular river scenery; another leads across flower-filled meadows, while the third offers superb views of mountains and a gorge torn open by the flood waters of Roaring River.

To reach the northeast corner of the park, take U.S. 34 or U.S. 36 to Estes Park. The trailheads are far enough apart to require separate instructions on how to reach them - and these will be given under the corresponding hike descriptions.

Cub Lake

Trailhead (1):	Cub Lake Trailhead
Distance one way:	2.3 miles
Altitude gain:	540 feet
Elevation at destination:	8,620 feet

Among the short and easy trails in the park, this is a favorite. This hike offers marvelous river scenery, exceptionally flowery meadows, superb stands of pine and aspen, and features a serenely beautiful lake backed by mountains at its destination.

To reach the trailhead from the Beaver Meadows entrance, follow the Bear Lake Road south for 1.2 miles; then turn right (west) toward the Moraine Park Campground. The turnoff is close to a side road to the left that leads uphill to the Moraine Park Visitor Center. After 0.7 miles turn left and follow the signs to Cub Lake and Fern Lake.

The trailhead parking lot has few spaces, and during the peak of the season is usually full by midmorning. If you're closed out of this lot, you can continue along the road to the Fern Lake parking area — no great disaster, but this will add about 1 mile to each direction if you walk back to the Cub Lake Trailhead by the path paralleling the road. Alternatively, taking the Fern Lake Trail to The Pool and then to Cub Lake will add 1.7 miles to the trip in each direction — an option that offers some lovely riverside views at the expense of foregoing the Cub Lake Trail altogether — it gets you to the lake, but it's not a fair tradeoff. Even this strategy is not failsafe: although the Fern Lake parking area is considerably larger, it is often filled by 10 a.m.

The trail begins with a sequence of bridges, the largest crossing the Big Thompson River. To the right (west) the scene is staged by a dramatic backdrop of mountains, to the left the river meanders through a valley filled with grasses and wildflowers. Marshy areas and small ponds border the river; alder, shrubby willows, and red-ozier dogwood cover the banks. Cow parsnip — what an ugly name for such a bold and beautiful plant — puts on a show for most of the summer with its huge maplelike leaves and showy flat heads of white blossoms. Shooting stars and lady-tresses orchid have a more delicate beauty. Although not as common, they too can be easily searched out along the banks.

The trail then leads across a broad valley covered with grass sporting feathery seed heads and autumn tints of beige and bronze by mid-July. The mountains create a distant blue-purple backdrop for the next act of

Cub Lake

the flower show: yarrow, black-eyed susan, coneflower, blanket flower, bee's balm, monk's hood, erigeron, fireweed, campanula, an occasional brilliant orange wood lily, and dozens of other flowers spark color onto the meadows. Huge lichen-covered erratics and rock outcroppings counterpoint the softness of the grasses, while groups of ponderosa pine add drama to the scene.

Gradually, the small stands of pine give way to larger ones, and these merge into an extensive forest. But here and there the pine is interrupted by fine stands of aspen that color reliably each fall. Many of these glens are carpeted by pteridium ferns, simultaneously bold and refined, and these too are painted gold by the chill of autumn — the entire color scheme set off by black-green conifers, dark rock, shadowed hills, and distant mountains.

A short and gentle climb brings you to the lake itself, bordered on two sides by a sea of undulating grass, rimmed by boulders on the opposite shore, and backed to the west by Stones Peak. Where the surface of the lake is clear it reflects the sky and mountains; elsewhere it is patched with yellow pond-lilly, the floating leaves studded here and there with large, goblet-shaped golden blooms.

The path continues along the north shore of the lake, ascending to give a fine overview before entering forest on the way to The Pool where it joins the Fern Lake Trail.

Big Thompson River near trailhead

Aspen, one of several spectacular stands along this trail

Cub Lake in winter

Cub Lake in Winter

Hiking the Cub Lake Trail in winter brings its own special rewards. Few trails offer such dramatic contrasts: frozen rivers have the glint of pewter; and the long, sun-drenched valley near the start of the trail is filled with fine-twigged shrubby willows, back-lit to a bronzy red haze and set against the dark backdrop of shadowed mountains. Farther on, the ponderosa pines stand alone or in small groups, black against the snow. Farther still are those wonderful stands of aspen — the trees side-lit stilettoes of white and pale gray-green, highlighted against the mountains and a sky of deeper hue than at any other season. A few hundred yards more brings you to the lake, still imposing against its mountain backdrop, even as a desolate expanse of gray ice.

Although this is a short and easy trail, there are a few winter annoyances. Part of the trail, particularly the initial third, is open to wind and is often snow-free and rocky — so skis and snowshoes have to be carried. On the other hand, some sections near the beginning are often covered by snow drifts, and one has to take care not to lose the path, particularly on the way back. The extra caution is a minor demand, considering what this trail has to offer.

Fern Falls and Fern Lake

Trailhead (2):	Fern Lake Trailhead
Distance one way:	2.7 miles (falls); 3.8 miles (lake)
Altitude gain:	650 feet (falls); 1,380 feet (lake)
Elevation at destination:	8,800 feet (falls); 9,530 feet (lake)

Those partial to water features in the landscape will find that this trail has it all — superb river scenery, interesting pools, an impressive water-fall, and a magnificent subalpine lake backed by mountains. Add to this some curious rock formations, extensive fern gardens, rare wildflowers, and dense forests carpeted with grouseberry, and it's easy to understand the popularity of this hike.

To reach the trailhead from the Beaver Meadows entrance, follow the route to Cub Lake (see p. 86), but continue on for an additional mile. Again, the size of the parking lot does not reflect the popularity of the hike, and it may be filled by midmorning during the summer months.

The trail is fairly level for the first mile or so, closely following the Big Thompson River upstream. All sorts of moisture-loving plants thrive along the banks. Besides elder, alder, cottonwood, and willows, there are superb clumps of mountain maple and river birch, the latter with polished red stems more like that of a cherry tree than a birch. And here is where you find ferns in such abundance as to justify the name of the lake, the falls, and the trail itself. Pteridium ferns cover the ground by the acre — a three-season treat, but particularly spectacular when autumn tints them gold in concert with the maple, birch, and alder.

About 1 mile from the trailhead, the path leads through a strange group of boulders — Arch Rocks — red in color, standing on end, maybe 30 feet high but with a bit of a tilt. It's a startling formation, completely incongruous with the surroundings.

The Pool

Another half-mile leads to a bridge that crosses the Big Thompson River. Here the trail splits; the left (east-heading) branch goes on to Cub Lake. Nearby, Fern Creek and Spruce Creek join the Big Thompson, and the water flows through a basin it cut for itself deep in the rock. This is The Pool. You see it first and most closely from the bridge; but then the trail climbs to a rocky ledge that gives you a more dramatic view.

Fern Lake in front of Notchtop Mountain and Little Matterhorn

The beginning of the trail features extensive stands of ferns

Passage through the Red Rocks

Fern Falls

Leaving The Pool, the trail becomes steeper, and the terrain more open, but with occasional jumbles of blocky, black granite boulders. When you again enter the forest, it's predominantly coniferous — mostly fir and spruce. Then, after 2.7 miles, the trail reaches Fern Falls. It's a bit unkempt, cluttered with enough boulders and fallen trees to make it as much a cascades as a falls, emphasizing the power of rushing water.

Close to the falls, just off the trail, is a grotto — shady and damp with a lush growth of cow parsnip and grasses on its floor. The black rock walls, slick with moisture, support a hanging garden complete with mosses, ferns, and sedges. The grotto is a small feature, but well worth a closer look before going on.

Fern Lake

The last mile climbs steadily through coniferous forest. Extensive patches of grouseberry carpet the floor and color early in shades of yellow, red, and orange, often nicely set off by the silvery trunks of downed trees.

The approach to the lake is marshy, the shore supporting some fine stands of elegant grass. A rock outcropping sits half in and half out of the water — there's room enough for a party of four, but you have to arrive early enough to be part of that party. Other dry perches can be found by going along its east shore.

Fern Creek has its outlet on the eastern shore where a bridge spanning the wet areas continues the trail that leads to Odessa Lake. Golden-twigged willows and red-ozier dogwoods back the bridge on all sides, giving the scene an impressionistic quality — the effect counterpointed by the rugged peaks of Little Matterhorn and Notchtop Mountain forming a backdrop to the southwest. It's a dramatic contrast that accounts for a great deal of the lake's character and appeal.

Gem Lake

Trailhead (3):	Gem Lake Trailhead. Exit off the U.S. 34 Bypass of Estes Park onto MacGregor Avenue, turn right before entering MacGregor Ranch and procede about ¾ mile to parking area on left.
Distance one way:	2 miles
Altitude gain:	1,090 feet
Elevation at destination:	8,830 feet

Some hikers belittle Gem Lake for its picayunish size (0.2 acre) and piddling depth (about 5 feet), ranking it as a semi-precious gem among the royal collection of lakes that grace the park. But this is pure slander, for what it lacks in size it makes up for in beauty, and the trail takes you up Lumpy Ridge through some of the most varied and distinctive scenery in the park — all for a mere 2-mile effort.

There is a choice of two trailheads that give access to the lake: Twin Owls on the MacGregor Ranch within park property, and the Gem Lake Trailhead off Devil's Gulch Road (which continues MacGregor Avenue) on private grounds. The first is a tad shorter and involves a bit less of a climb, but the parking lot can be full by 10 a.m. since the area is a mecca for rock climbers. So it is often less of a hassle to start from the second trailhead, and this is where our description begins.

The first 0.8 miles of this route leads through private land where barbed-wire fencing enforces 'No Trespassing' signs. But even this part of the trail is interesting, where envy-provoking homesites stake out acres of wildflowers. Violet monarda, blue erigeron, yellow senecio, and white achillea are among the most common; but many others are also abundant.

Then the grade becomes steeper, and short switchbacks take you to ever lumpier regions of Lumpy Ridge. Near the 1-mile mark the path splits — the left (west) branch leading to the Twin Owls Trailhead, the right goes northeast to Gem Lake.

The path continues on a more moderate grade through open forest of ponderosa pine. Huge and bizarre outcroppings of rock dominate a scene reminiscent of the stone chessmen that characterize Bryce Canyon in Utah, except that these pieces are dark gray granite, not red sandstone. Here and there side trails invite you to explore these formations. Don't

Boulders carved by the elements into freeform sculpture

View of Estes Park from Gem Lake Trail

Gem Lake

miss the opportunity — it's like strolling through a stone sculpture garden, plus there are grand views of Estes Park and other sections of Lumpy Ridge.

Past the midway mark the path enters a more heavily forested area — aspen, pine, spruce, and fir shade the way. Soon the forest opens, again revealing spectacular views of Estes Park and the ridge. Then the trail ascends more quickly by short, steep switchbacks, and in a few minutes delivers you to lakeside.

That first view is quite special. The lake is set in an amphitheater — a wall of stone, perhaps 50 feet high, begins on your right and half circles the lake along its east shore. Parts of the wall are so steep that technical rock climbers are often seen honing their skills here. On the left (west), rock ledges and a good-sized sandy beach provide perfect seats for the spectators.

True, the lake is small and shallow. True, its popularity guarantees that you will have company. And yes, a herd of horses may stop for lunch when you do. But this is a highly scenic hike, the views are spectacular, the setting of the lake is beautiful, and the rock formations are as unusual as any that can be seen in the park — all within a couple of miles of trailhead.

Ypsilon Lake

Trailhead (4):	Lawn Lake Trailhead
Distance one way:	4.5 mile
Altitude gain:	2,180 feet
Elevation at destination:	10,540 feet

Ypsilon Lake takes its name from the mountain that towers above its northwest shore to an elevation of 13,514 feet. Its precipitous southeast face, scarred by a snow-packed, Y-shaped couloir, makes it one of the most distinctive and formidable peaks in the park. In addition to the lake and the spectacular views of its namesake mountain, this trail offers several other rewards: a visit to Chipmunk Lake, a tarn of lesser size but no lesser beauty; well-composed scenes of Longs Peak; pine forests carpeted with grouseberry, juniper, and bearberry; and dramatic views of the canyon gouged out by rampaging water that broke loose from Lawn Lake Dam in 1982 and flowed down the Roaring River.

Trailhead parking has room for a few dozen cars, the exact number depending on the considerateness of those who arrived earlier. Serving

Ypsilon Lake with Mount Chiquita as a backdrop

Chipmunk Lake reflecting Ypsilon Mountain

both the Lawn Lake and the Ypsilon Lake trails, the lot is popular enough to fill by 9 a.m. on summer weekends.

The hike begins with a series of switchbacks. After about 0.5 miles the trail passes along the rim of the canyon cut by the flood water of Lawn Lake. It's hard to imagine that the modest stream seen meandering at the bottom could be charged to such destructive force as to tear open this vast rent in the hillside, and carry away trees, boulders, and an enormous tonnage of earth that restricted its former course. The vast alluvial fan of mud and sand that was swept down the hillside into Horseshoe Park is still mostly barren.

Nearing the 1.3-mile mark, the Lawn Lake Trail branches off to the right, and then the Ypsilon Lake Trail crosses Roaring River by way of a log bridge. The first view of Ypsilon Mountain appears in the background to the northwest.

The trail again takes up the ascent in earnest through steep switchbacks secured by log steps. Lodgepole pine dominates the forest as the trail climbs and moderates, climbs and moderates, over the better part of 2.5 miles. About 4 miles from trailhead the path begins to descend and the forest opens to reveal a spectacular view of Ypsilon Mountain, its extraordinary southeast face and the full extent of its Y-shaped gash straight ahead and fully visible.

Soon you are at the southwest shore of Chipmunk Lake. A few steps to the marshy southeast side garners a great view of Ypsilon Mountain and its lake-reflected image. This is a small lake, a mere 0.1 acre in surface area, but it makes a big impression with pale tan boulders de-lineating its northwest shore, moss and sedge carpeting the southeast shore, and the magnificent mountain backdrop. It's difficult to leave, but Ypsilon Lake is still 0.5 miles away.

The trail now descends steeply from a well-defined lateral moraine, climbs a bit on the other side, and then descends steeply to Ypsilon Lake, passing the cascades of a stream emanating from Chiquita Lake. You meet Ypsilon Lake with dramatic suddenness at its western edge, and the drama increases as you continue along its southern boundary.

The precipitous rise of Ypsilon Mountain from the northwest shore of the lake provides a spectacular backdrop, but crops the view of the southeast face. The trail skirts the lake along three-quarters of its shore, and many short spurs lead to the water's edge providing private places for lunch and a snooze.

Ypsilon Mountain from the trail

Deer Mountain

Trailhead (5):	Dear Ridge Junction Trailhead near the junction of Colorado 34 and Colorado 36
Distance one way:	3 miles
Altitude gain:	1,080 feet
Elevation at destination:	10,010 feet

This pleasant hike leads from flowery meadows and open stands of pine, up through conifer-wooded switchbacks to the top of Deer Mountain. Along the way and on the summit, there are excellent views of Ypsilon Mountain, Longs Peak, and Estes Park.

The trail is gently ascending for the first mile, and this section offers some of the best scenery. Near the beginning of the hike, looking to the northwest, you see Ypsilon Mountain framed by ponderosa pine. The snow-filled, Y-shaped gash on the mountains southeast face makes it easy to recognize. A bit farther on, the forest gives way to grass-covered slopes with a few isolated pines of impressive size here and there.

Looking south to Longs Peak from the summit of Deer Mountain

Aspen and Longs Peak seen from the trail

Wildflowers, in abundance and variety, mingle with the grasses.
Before walking a mile, you reach a grove of aspen extending downhill to the south. Beaver Meadows fills the middle of the scene, while Longs Peak, 9 miles farther south, forms the backdrop. It's a superb view.

Past this point, the trail makes a sharp switchback, and begins to climb more steeply up the southern flank of Deer Mountain and into a coniferous forest. For most of the second mile, pines and fir shade the trail, but there are several turnouts which provide excellent views of the valleys below and the surrounding mountains.

With less than a mile to go, the grade moderates to level, and then to a gentle downhill slope. Then the trail becomes sandy and indistinct. The forest is more open here, exposing some local highpoints, but not the summit of Deer Mountain.

A pyramidal cairn of monumental size marks a splitting of the path 0.1 miles from the summit. The branch to follow makes a right-angle right and heads steeply upward over rock and scree, some of which is not too firmly anchored.

At the top of Deer Mountain ancient limber pines and picturesque snags testify to the harshness of mountain weather even at a mere 10,000 feet. You can use the trees to frame excellent views of Estes Park to the east, Longs Peak to the south, and Ypsilon Mountain to the northwest. There are all sorts of flat-topped boulders to serve as benches or tables when you're ready for lunch.

Old Ute Trail - Trail Ridge to Beaver Meadows

Trailhead (6):	Old Ute Trailhead on Trail Ridge Rd., 2.0 miles west of Rainbow Curve, 0.8 miles east of Forest Canyon Overlook
Distance one way:	6.1 miles (suggested one way route using 2 cars)
Altitude loss:	3,000 feet
Elevation at start:	11,250 feet

The Old Ute Trail was part of an Indian route that once linked villages across the Continental Divide. In its 3,000-foot elevation drop, the section of the trail described here passes through three mountain zones: alpine, subalpine, and montane. Although several of the other hikes do the same, none is shorter, and none offers a greater variety of plant environments.

Stepping onto the tundra at 11,250 feet, is like setting foot on some strange planet — a vast, alien, and desolate landscape. You're Gulliver in the gardens of Lilliput, wandering among windwise miniature plants less than ankle high. What they lack in size they make up for in floriferousness — saxifrage, silene, phlox, and sedum, completely mantle themselves in bloom through most of July and August.

The first 2 miles of trail are gently hilly, providing excellent views across Forest Canyon to the Continental Divide. Longs Peak stands sentinel to the south. Wherever the trail offers a sweeping view, Longs will be a prominent feature on the horizon. After a climb of 200 feet, the descent begins, at first gradually. Here, potentilla steals the show — the 2-foot shrubs covering extensive patches of tundra in golden flowers. Here too, are excellent views to the south into the Fern Lake area.

Then the trail begins to descend more steeply, and it will get steeper still. Since the upper third is level to gently ascending, and the lower third is gently rolling to level, most of the altitude loss accurs while decending the middle third — not too bad going downhill, but going up this part of the Old Ute Trail is best left to young Utes.

The start of the steep descent presents a superb view of the route down to Upper Beaver Meadows; the enormous lateral moraine that

Near the start of the hike, Longs Peak in the background

shoulders the trail over much of its last half is a dominant feature. A few hundred steps leads to a chest-high forest of subalpine fir — Krummholtz, sculpted and sheared by the winds and snow. Further along the trail the trees are taller, and near the 2.5-mile mark is an open stand of limber pines. The trees are large, old, and twisted — some scarred by fire, others flayed of bark to their silvery core over most of their trunk.

Continuing its steep descent through dense forest of pine and fir, the path occasionally opens onto a meadow awash with wildflowers. These are not the tight, frugal knots of the tundra, but a luxuriance of full-sized plants — scarlet paintbrush, purple penstemon, white achillea, and many others in mixtures that would embarrass a necktie — but here just perfect.

Further on, the grade begins to moderate. In places where the spruce and fir are spaced more widely, juniper spreads over the ground, creating the illusion of a well-manicured garden. A sign gives the distance and direction to the Upper Beaver Meadows Trailhead, 2.8 miles ahead. Again the plant community changes: violet monarda and golden gallardia best our cultivated ones; allium and erigeron, blackeyed susan and golden banner vie for attention; but the exquisite mariposa lily takes center stage.

The rushing water of Windy Gulch Creek is heard long before it is seen; but then it comes within a few feet of the trail before cascading out of sight to the valley below. The trail continues over rock ledges that provide a wonderful view of the valley below. Then the path levels out through dense forest of lodgepole pine interspersed with superb stands of aspen. Of course, there are more flowers — the display continuing right into the parking area.

Near the lower trailhead you will notice a large area enclosed by a fence. The purpose of the fence is to exclude deer and elk. This is part of an experiment to study the kind of plant growth that occurs in an area protected from foraging.

There are several variations on this hike. Those with a surplus of energy will insist on doing it from the bottom up, or use only one car and travel the trail both directions. But others can simply hike a bit of the top or a bit of the bottom, and return to the same trailhead. It will do, but it's second best to walking the entire trail and experiencing the rich variety of landscapes it has to offer.

Bush cinquefoil in full bloom on the alpine tundra

Chapin, Chiquita, and Ypsilon Mountains

Trailhead (7):	Chapin Creek Trailhead
Distance one way:	1.5 miles (Mt. Chapin), 2.4 miles (Mt. Chiquita), and 3.5 miles (Mt. Ypsilon)
Altitude gain:	1,814 feet; 2,429 feet; and 2,874 feet respectively
Elevation at destination:	12,454 feet; 13,069 feet; and 13,514 feet respectively

This is a tour of three mountain peaks — two of which top out at over 13,000 feet. Much of the trail is on alpine tundra above timberline, and there are marvelous views of the Chapin Creek Valley and the Mummy Range along the way. But the most spectacular views of all are those seen from the three summits. From each you can see the precipitous east face of at least one of the others and Horseshoe Park and Estes Park far below to the southeast.

To reach the trailhead from the Beaver Meadows entrance, drive northwest on U.S. 36 to Deer Ridge Junction. Continue northwest (bearing right), now on U.S. 34 headed for Endovalley. Past Endovalley, the paved road ends, and you continue on the one-way-only Fall River Road — rutty, dusty, and replete with hairpin curves for its 8.5 mile stretch to the Alpine Visitor Center. The 15 mph speed limit is none too conservative. The trailhead is reached about 6.5 miles from Endovalley, and will be on your right. There are parking spaces on the left in a small parking area and along the shoulder of the road.

For the first quarter of a mile, the trail climbs steeply to a ridge, and then turns sharply right (east). The path leads through a dense forest of spruce and fir. After about a mile, the trees are shorter, and the forest begins to open. On your left (to the north) is a view down into the Chapin Creek Valley, where the river is a band of silver twisting through a generous border of bright green grass strikingly framed by the conifer-covered mountains.

Soon the trail climbs above timberline, where the view is truly expansive. As you proceed across the western flank of Mount Chapin, the

Ypsilon Mountain from Trail Ridge Road

trail crosses fingers of talus, and here is where you discover the worth of hiking boots with good support, good ankle protection, and sturdy soles.

The trail becomes indistinct, then imaginary. An ascent of a few hundred feet takes you to the summit of Mount Chapin with its remarkable views of Chiquita and the valleys to the southeast. Some, preferring a shorter hike, make this their destination, and then turn back.

Those going on to the other peaks cross the saddle between Mounts Chapin and Chiquita. Here, for the first time, you see the east face of both of these mountains, the precipitous drop in sharp contrast to the moderate western slopes.

Improvise a route to the summit of Chiquita. Much of the walk will be across talus, not the most comfortable of walking surfaces. Situated at the top is a small, rock amphitheater. Partly the work of people, but mostly that of nature, it faces eastward — a perfect place to enjoy a snack and the dramatic views of the companion mountains.

Then it's on to Ypsilon Mountain, descending a few hundred feet to the Ypsilon-Chiquita saddle before climbing the southern peak of Ypsilon. This peak offers the best view of Ypsilon's dramatic east face with its snow-filled couloirs, but the northern peak, a short walk across a shallow saddle, gives the best view of Spectacle Lakes.

One can continue mountain hopping along the Mummy Range to Fairchild Mountain and Hagues Peak, both thirteeners. However, this extends the hike way beyond the limits of the trails covered here, and the Lawn Lake Trail provides a more convenient route. Besides, the view from Ypsilon Mountain deserves a long and leisurely stay, and there is scenery enough along the way to satisfy the most discriminating hiker.

Ypsilon Mountain's northeast peak seen from its southeast peak

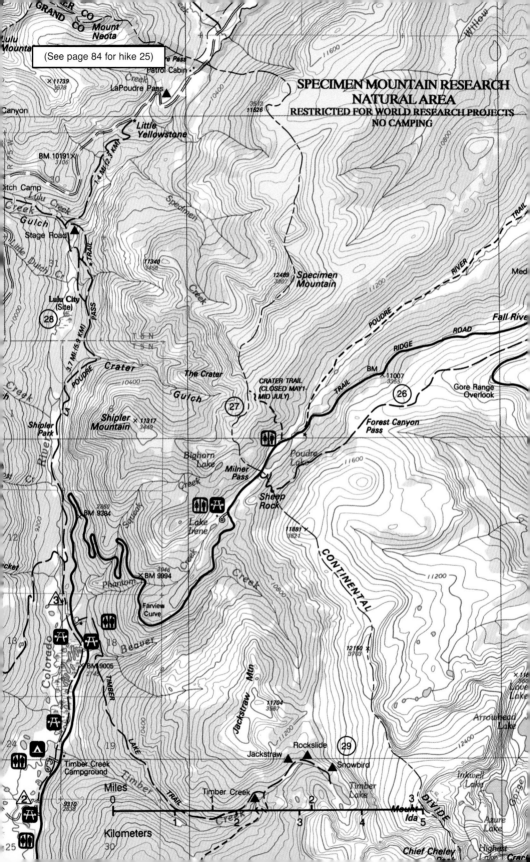

NORTHWEST
Trails Near Poudre Lake

25 — Short tundra hikes

26 — Old Ute Trail - Trail Ridge Road to Poudre Lake

27 — The Crater

28 — Lulu City and Little Yellowstone Canyon

29 — Timber Lake

Since this region of the park includes a section of the Continental Divide, it is not surprising that many of the best alpine tundra hikes are found here. The other trails included here lie to the west of the Divide, where moisture is more abundant. These trails feature gentle marshes, lush forests, superb river scenery, and tranquil lakes.

All these trails are reached from the northwest section of Trail Ridge Road. During winter, when the northern section of the road is closed, only the Timber Lake and Colorado River trails can be reached, and then only by traveling north on Trail Ridge Road from Grand Lake.

Short Tundra Hikes

Trailhead (1):	Tundra Trail Trailhead on Trail Ridge Road; (2): Trail Ridge Road opposite Alpine Visitor Center; (3): Alpine Visitor Center
Distance:	A few steps to a few miles — customize to suit
Altitude gain:	Nominal to negative
Elevation at trailhead:	About 11,500 feet

The alpine tundra is another world perched on the penthouse of the planet where living is anything but posh and easy. It's a land of raging winds, fearsome electrical storms, and a nine-month winter of bitter cold and heavy snow. Yet it's home to creatures like the marmot and pika, and all sorts of miniature plants whose delicate form and exquisite blossoms are in sharp contrast to the harshness of the setting. Flowery throughout the summer, the show is at its height from mid-July to mid-August, with an encore of more subtle beauty beginning in early September when bright blossoms give way to rich tints of amber and russet.

And the views — Ah! the views! — Spectacular in almost every direction.

For much of the summer the alpine tundra is usually sun-soaked in the morning and overcast in the afternoon. The clouds often bring rain — not gentle showers, but thunderstorms that demand attention and respect. Even under clear skies the temperature can be 30o cooler than in Estes Park, and wind is likely to be a brisk and badgering presence throughout the day — annoying to some, but for others adding to the sense of place and excitement.

All the walks described here begin at Trail Ridge Road — topping out at over 12,000 feet, it's the highest continuous road in the U.S., and most of its northern stretch reaches above timberline.

Perhaps the most popular is the 0.3-mile hike that starts at the parking lot serving the Alpine Visitor Center. The climb is short but steep, and at the top are the expected grand views and an alpine garden featuring all sorts of hummocky plants set against white, quartz-laced boulders and scree. A sign informs you that the elevation is higher than the summit of Mount Hood.

Mushroom-shaped rock on Tundra Trail

Nearly as popular is the Tundra Trail, which begins just west of Rock Cut on Trail Ridge Road. The parking area is fairly generous, but still likely to be at or near capacity on a clement weekend afternoon during summer. A commodious outhouse at the trailhead may be momentarily as welcome a sight as the spectacular scenery. The half-mile hike climbs gradually to several extraordinary rock outcroppings, one featuring a carbuncle of stone some 15 feet high, bizarre but beautiful, incongruously rising out of the tundra like a mushroom. A bit further on, defining the end of the walk for most people, is a fortresslike stone outcropping — a striking view in itself and providing striking views for those who scramble to its top.

Two hikes incorporating portions of the Old Ute Trail are described on pages 102 and 112, where a two-car shuttle is suggested in order to avoid retracing the route. But you can enjoy both of these trails by walking the tundra portion and returning to the upper trailhead, and neither is likely to be as crowded as the other two described here.

Although none of the four tundra hikes mentioned in this section are of day length, one can customize a day-long trip by doing several in succession — it's a treat. Take care to stay on the paths; in spite of the ruggedness of the terrain and the harshness of the climate, this is an extremely fragile ecosystem, one that is easy to wound and slow to heal.

Old Ute Trail - Trail Ridge to Poudre Lake

Trailhead (2):	Trail Ridge Road across from the Alpine Visitor Center
Distance one way:	4.2 miles
Altitude loss:	1,050 feet
Elevation at start:	11,800 feet

This is another section of the Old Ute Trail (see p. 102) which can be traversed in one direction by arranging a two-car shuttle. As expected of a trail that starts in the alpine zone and ends well into the subalpine, this hike passes through a rich variety of landscapes, from the austere beauty of the tundra, to lush forests of fir, to the hanging gardens near Poudre Lake. No trail surpasses this one in its abundance and diversity of wildflowers.

Alpine tundra near the start of the hike

Hanging Lake

The upper trailhead is on Trail Ridge Road directly across from the east entrance of the parking lot that serves the Alpine Visitor Center. The trailhead is not marked at this writing, but is easily located.

For about a third of its length the path leads through treeless tundra carpeted with miniature alpine plants: saxifrage, phlox, silene, sedum, mountain dryad, alpine sunflower, as well as globeflower and elephantella which one usually associates with wetter terrain and lower altitudes. Throughout this part of the hike there are superb views of the mountains defining the Continental Divide.

At about the 1-mile mark is a series of pools, hanging lakes if they were larger, perched above valleys at the very rim of the dropoff. Sedges and grasses grow abundantly on the shores creating minimarshes that seem out of place in the alpine tundra.

So gradual is the descent that the introduction of trees into the landscape is almost imperceptible. First, ground-hugging colonies of subalpine fir appear; then bolder, isolated stands studded with pennant trees; then larger stands with short but properly cone-shaped sentinels in the center; and finally, subalpine forest with full-sized spruce and fir.

Rock spires and hanging gardens near Poudre Lake

Poudre Lake

The wildflowers reflect the change in altitude, shade, and moisture — the alpine miniatures give way to blue chiming bell, white phlox-like bittercress, penstemon, beesbalm, indian paintbrush, lady tresses orchid, and many more.

About two-thirds of a mile from the lake, a rocky outcrop presents a garden of silver-leaved and golden-flowered senecio, purple-plumed silky phacelius, penstemon, and anaphalis — but wait, the best is up ahead. Another half mile leads to a startling outcrop of rock pinnacles. Saxafrage, heuchera, sedum, and many other alpine miniatures spread out on the prominences or nestle in the cracks — an exquisite hanging garden made even more striking by the patches of orange lichen that decorate the rock. Although only a few hundred yards from Poudre Lake, it's an apt reward for a much longer hike.

Poudre Lake is bordered by Trail Ridge Road and is served by a fairly large parking lot, providing convenient access to the lake. Many visitors, having only one car at their disposal, choose to hike the lower portion of the trail starting from the lake. Others come to stroll along the southeast shore where it's easy to find a pleasant spot to stop for lunch.

The Crater

Trailhead (4):	Crater Trailhead at Milner Pass
	near Poudre Lake
Distance one way:	1 mile
Altitude gain:	730 feet
Elevation at destination:	11,480 feet

The trail to The Crater is only a mile long, but steep enough to make it more than a casual stroll. The hike begins in dense forest and ends above timberline at the rim of an enormous concavity like the crater of a volcano. If you're lucky you will see bighorn sheep, but no luck is needed to enjoy the grand view. Considering the popularity of the hike, the parking area at trailhead is skimpy, and you might have to park a few hundred feet away at Poudre Lake and walk back along the road — if so watch out for cars whose drivers are watching out for scenery.

The Crater and the 1,000-foot rise of Specimen Mountain above its rim is a bighorn sheep sanctuary, off limits to hikers. It's a good guess that many take this trail primarily in hopes of seeing sheep. But seldom is a large congregation spotted, and thundering herds are out of the question. Expect to see a small group here and there, and on some days none at all.

But it's not only the sheep that distinguish this hike. The trail passes through beautiful subalpine forest of spruce, the ground covered with extensive patches of grouseberry that turn coppery red in autumn. The forest ends quite suddenly, opening up an expansive view of the Poudre River Valley. The river is strikingly set-off by a border of bright green vegetation — a striking contrast to the dark green conifers that cover the surrounding hills. The trail continues its steep climb, and soon reaches the rim of the Crater.

The scene is also a striking study in contrasts — dark conifers cover the east-facing slopes, while the west-facing slopes show only the light tan color of bare rock. Across The Crater to the west, the Never Summer Range dominates the horizon. Rising above The Crater to the north is Specimen Mountain, a web of game trails crisscrossing its flanks from its summit down to the bottom of The Crater. Some of these trails are used by the bighorns; all are off limits to hikers since Specimen Mountain is designated as a "National Research Area" that can only be visited by researchers with a special permit.

Looking down into The Crater

Specimen Mountain is named for the abundance of interesting rock specimens to be found on its slopes — found, but hopefully left in place, since this is a park for all of us. Once thought to be an active volcano that blew its top, geologists now believe that the ash deposits on Specimen, as well as other features of volcanic origin, like the Lava Cliffs a few miles east, came from volcanic activity that occurred outside the park. The crater is merely the result of erosion. While the latest theory robs the site of some of its romantic aura, it does nothing to diminish its scenic impact.

Lulu City and Little Yellowstone Canyon

Trailhead (5):	Colorado River Trailhead, northwest corner of Trail Ridge Road
Distance one way:	3.7 miles (Lulu City); 4.6 miles (Little Yellowstone Canyon)
Altitude gain:	350 feet (Lulu City); 990 feet (Little Yellowstone Canyon)
Elevation at destination:	9,360 feet (Lulu City); 10,000 feet (Little Yellowstone Canyon)

The Colorado River Trail is your route to Lulu City, once a mining town built in the hope of striking it rich in gold and silver. After Lulu City, the trail continues for an additional 0.7 miles to the Little Yellowstone Canyon. Along the way, you get to enjoy excellent river scenery, lush marshlands, and pleasant forests. All of which makes this a varied and interesting trail in every season of the year.

Former site of Lulu City

The Colorado River as seen near the beginning of the trail

Some of the most impressive scenery occurs within the first half mile, where the path and the river run closely parallel to each other. Elder, alder, willows, and grasses soften sections of the bank; bare pebbles cobble other sections; spruce encroach upon the shore, lean precariously out over the water and then bend backward as though having thought better of it. The river is the Colorado — most impressive during the late spring runoff, but always a scenic highpoint.

The trail follows the river upstream a bit, and then, too soon, diverges from it and leads through open forest of mixed trees. One extensive stand of aspen is backed by a cliff, and the gray-black rock makes a perfect foil for the white trunks. Further on is a marsh with billowing clumps of grass and many small ponds interconnected by a system of rivulets. Beyond the bright green of the marsh are hills covered with somber blue-green conifers; beyond the hills, the snow-capped, gray mountains.

Soon the workings of man come into evidence in the mountain side to the right of the trail. The tailing of the Shipler Mine still litter the slope after a hundred years; tons of cracked rock turned out of the mountain in search of ounces of silver. It's a half mile further along the trail to the Shipler cabins, two broken down one-roomers slowly being reclaimed by the forest. Joe Shipler built the first cabin in 1876. After thirty-eight years, rheumatic and not much richer, he abandoned the mine and left the valley.

Tailings from the Shipler Mine

A few steps past these cabins and a few steps into the woods at the left of the trail is another wooden cabin, this one of more modern origin, and still in use — an outhouse, unremarkable except for its convenience.

After leaving the Shipler cabins, the trail leads through denser forest, again conifers and aspen, but now the conifers predominate. The trail becomes more hilly, more gravelly, but the inclines are moderate and short. Soon the path leads out onto a flat grassy expanse, set parklike among well-forested hills and the mountains. You have arrived. This is the site of Lulu City. The mining town that sprang up like a mushroom in 1879, collapsed some five years later — not enough pay dirt to make it pay. However, at the height of its gold fever, it boasted a hotel, post office, biweekly stagecoach, and even a brothel — a Rocky Mountain winter can be long and cold.

A couple of collapsed cabins front the entrance to the nearly vanished town; their new occupants are spruce trees, outgrowing their welcome and about to assimilate their hosts. A quarter of a mile uptrail, near the end of the townsite, a coppice of spruce is skirted by the remains of another cabin, now reduced to a four-log-high tree planter. Aside from the three broken-down cabins, other signs of Lulu City are hard to find in this gentle field — the forest has absorbed almost all of it. However, it is easy to find the modern cabin to the east of the trail — it's another outhouse.

I wonder if Shipler and the citizens of Lulu City appreciated the wondrous beauty around them; or were they too entranced with the quest for precious metal to give a damn. Maybe the platinum hoarfrost, the ice-silvered streams, the aspen's autumn gold only served to remind them of the impending winter and the past season's stingy issue of real gold and silver. What was it like to endure the fierce summer storms, the hail, and lightning? How did they cope with the winter snows driven by raging 80 mph winds, and the bone-cracking chill of 30° below. There seems to be no limit to the privation and suffering people willingly endure for the sake of accumulating enough wealth to avoid such privation and suffering. We come to hike in the most pleasant weather and leave by day's end, but some of the inhabitants of Lulu stayed the year around. There's nothing like the promise of wealth to forge stoic resolve.

If you wish to hike farther than Lulu City, you can continue north to Little Yellowstone Canyon, an additional 0.9 miles with an elevation gain of 640 feet. There are two different routes. One continues through the meadow and is a bit less strenuous; the other branches off to the right just before you enter Lulu City and follows the La Poudre River Trail. After 0.6 miles, the two trails meet and gently descend to the Colorado River, at this point only a many-channeled hint of its later force and volume. Rustic bridges provide a crossing, and then you begin the modest ascent along the narrow gravelly path on the canyon wall.

Within a quarter-mile the canyon walls become more solid and blocky. Looking down into the canyon may call up images of the big Yellowstone Canyon in Wyoming — but here the scale is much reduced.

A trail for all seasons

The scenery along the Colorado River Trail changes dramatically throughout the year. Each season scripts its own scenario, and each scenario is wondrously different from the others.

Spring offers the river at its fullest and contrasts the newly minted leaves of the deciduous trees against slate gray rock or the somber gray-green of the conifers still in candle or, more vibrantly, against the unbeatable blue of a Colorado sky. Early wildflowers spark the fields, and the meadow grasses show the flounce and turgor of fresh new growth. In the background, steel blue mountains are still well-mantled with snow, just the backdrop for the bright fresh colors of the meadows and marshes. And the air . . . Perfect . . . Perfect in temperature . . . Not too dry, not too damp . . . And filled with the rich aroma of new growth and newly shed pine needles stirred up by thunderstorms that regularly punctuate late afternoons and evenings during this season.

Summer calms the landscape; anneals the soft spring rush of growth to hard wood; overpaints the lime green aspen leaves in low key but substantial blue-gray-greens, and whitens the bark; stiffens the candles of the conifers and brushes them out; plumes the many grasses with airy inflorescences; brings the wildflower show to a peak; but leaves enough snow on the mountains to remind you that there are other seasons.

Autumn is the most flamboyant time of the year. The landscape is reworked with a full palette: the entire spectrum of greens from blue to yellow show in the conifers; aspen sparkle yellow, gold, or even orange; grouseberry, a blueberry relative, carpets the forest floor with coppery scarlet; here and there sumacs of several species flare an incandescent ruby red on the hillsides. The grasses are more reserved, turning subtle shades of yellow, gold, bronze, and tan. The ponds, streams, and the Colorado River reflect the blue of the sky and mix this color among all the others tossed onto the water from the banks.

As autumn flames itself out, the aspen deciduate, and scatter their gold along the paths and into the water. All is unadorned structure, spare and elegant. Then the snows come, and the landscape takes its most dramatic turn, a change into its boldest form, simplified into steely contrasts. White skeletal aspen are set against gray-black rocks; rivers and pools appear black against snow-covered banks, as do the conifers under their white topcoats; and even the mountains seem black where free of snow. Only the sky gives color to this black and white scene, and this color is the deepest, purest blue of the season, unless a storm is brewing. But during a gentle snowfall, the harsh black-and- white contrast is gone, and in its place is a new, impressionistic landscape, with snow-dusted trees and rocks, and the misty hills and barely discernible mountains in the background.

And the winter visitor garners another bonus — solitude — few others will be there to disturb the tranquility. Snowshoes can be used, but this trail has so few steep sections, and these are so short, that even the near novice should have little trouble with it. It's mostly an easy skate up, and an almost continuous, gentle schuss down.

The winter route to Lulu City and Little Yellowstone Canyon is the same as the summer route — the Colorado River Trail. However, the parking lot serving that trailhead is not plowed, so leave your car at the Timber Lake parking lot, and ski west across the road. A signboard farther west at the bottom of a hill marks the beginning of the trail.

Since Trail Ridge Road is closed during winter, one has to come by way of the Grand Lake entrance, a two-hour drive from Boulder or Denver. However, the drive through Clear Creek Canyon is a scenic treat in itself, and the winter ski tour to Lulu City is unbeatable.

Timber Lake

Trailhead (6):	Timber Lake Trailhead on Trail Ridge Road 9.6 miles north of the Grand Lake entrance
Distance one way:	4.8 miles
Altitude gain:	2,060 feet
Elevation at destination:	11,060 feet

Most of the Timber Lake Trail passes through dense forest, so there are few sweeping views. On the other hand, the shade makes for pleasant hiking, and the trail boasts all sorts of water features and an exceptionally rich variety of woodland wildflowers. Located away from the more crowded sections of the park, this hike offers more tranquility and solitude than many others. The lake itself is a fine prize, beautifully set off by the mountains rising behind its southwest shore.

The beginning of the trail is graced by a large stand of aspen — mature trees, straight-trunked and tall — one of the finest groves in the park.

Timber Lake

Winter aspen

It's a treat in every season, but see it in the fall when it's in full incandescent shimmer, or in the winter when it's a white-on-white picture of bare trunks and snow.

Soon the path crosses Phantom Creek; then, after a third of a mile of fairly level terrain, leads to a bridge spanning a good-sized cascade churned up by Beaver Creek. Then the trail begins to climb more steeply through forest of lodgepole pine, spruce, and fir. You will hear the cars on Trail Ridge Road, but soon the noise gives way to the sound of water as you travel parallel to, but not in sight of, Timber Creek.

Near the 2-mile mark, you finally meet Timber Creek a few feet to the side of the trail, its banks garlanded with wildflowers — blue chiming bell is juxtaposed with white, phlox-like brook cress. Here and there, poised on boulders midstream, one sees magenta flowering clumps of the fabulous Parry primrose. The trail soon leaves the creek, then returns and leaves a few more times.

When 1.7 miles from the lake — a sign gives the direction and the distance — the path turns sharply left, and climbs by short switchbacks. This is the steepest portion of the trail, but it lasts only a quarter of a mile. Another half-mile or so leads to a rock outcropping heavily laced with quartz — the white of the boulders a striking foil for an extensive stand of scarlet indian paintbrush.

Soon the forest opens up to reveal a meadow skirting the southern flank of Jackstraw Mountain. A sign points the way to a strategically placed outhouse. Other signs point to this campground or that, and there is a turnoff to the right (south) to Long Meadows. Proceed northeast across the meadow to the clumpy subalpine forest at the far end.

After a few more steep switchbacks, the trail arrives at Timber Lake near the origin of Timber Creek. Here the shore is marshy, but replete with globe flower, marsh marigold, and superb clumps of the rare bog laurel clothed in three-quarter inch cotton-candy-pink hexagonal blooms for a month in early summer.

There are dry perches to be had on the northwest and southeast shores. The first is on boulders at the water's edge. The second, on a rise facing the Continental Divide, gives the best view — the lake set against a backdrop of mountains. There are several other scenic viewpoints, and many places where you can explore the shore.

Quartz-laced boulders within a half-mile of the lake

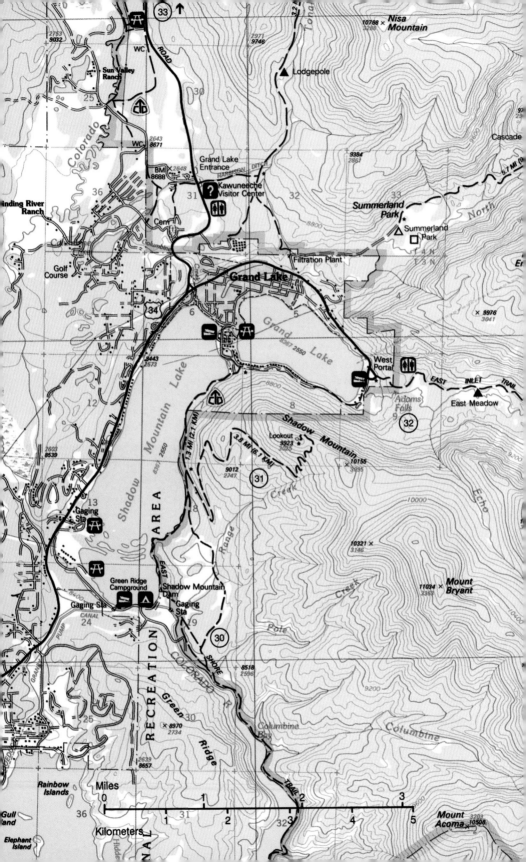

SOUTHWEST
Trails Near Grand Lake

30 — Columbine Bay
31 — Shadow Mountain
32 — Adams Falls
33 — Onahu - Tonahutu - Green Mountain Trail Loop

Some of Colorado's largest lakes border the southwest corner of the park, and the Colorado River passes through this region from north to south, gaining volume along the way. Added to these sources of moisture is that which is wrung from the clouds as they come in from the west and press up against the Continental Divide, making this the most verdant section of the park. There are excellent trails along lakeshores and the Colorado River, as well as mountain hikes and a hike to a pleasant waterfall. And since this region is 20 miles farther from Denver than the east side of the park, it draws fewer visitors, and so offers more solitude.

The area can be reached from the south by taking U.S. 40 to Granby, and from there taking U.S. 34 to Grand Lake. Trail Ridge Road is open from midspring to midautumn, and provides an alternate route to Grand Lake from the east side of the park.

127

Shadow Mountain Lake to Columbine Bay

Trailhead (1):	East Shore Trailhead via U.S. 34 in Grand Lake
Distance one way:	1.5 miles and beyond if you choose
Altitude gain:	nominal
Elevation at destination:	8,250 feet

This easy and pleasant trail from Shadow Mountain to Columbine Bay passes through a variety of riverside environments replete with gentle scenes of mountain-backed meadows, luxuriant marshes, and dense lodgepole forest. At the destination is a serenely beautiful bay. It's a hike for all seasons and a special treat for those with a penchant for river scenery.

The trailhead is reached by driving east on the 1.2-mile side road off of U.S. 34 near the center of Grand Lake's motel row. Park at the Green Ridge

Shadow Mountain Lake at twilight

Shadow Mountain Lake

Campground on the western side of Shadow Mountain Dam, and walk across the dam to the park boundary and trailhead on its eastern side.

On summer weekends the dam and the shores of its run-off are likely to be crowded by picnickers and fisherman, while the lake itself hosts a regatta of small sailboats, rowboats, and power boats. Nevertheless, the lake is magnificent, and the tree-studded rolling hills that form its shores and the mountain ranges behind them provide it with a magnificent setting. And after a few minutes on the trail, solitude is yours.

A short walk through pine forest leads to a marshy plain thick with grasses, bordered closely on one side by the Colorado River and on the other by hills, strangely dry and covered with yuccas and ghostly-gray sages. Then the plain extends its reach far to the east where it's backed by mountains. In spring and early summer, this part of the trail is boggy enough to warrant its wood-planked walkway, successfully designed to be as unobtrusive as possible. Between the last frosts of spring and before the first frosts of autumn this plain and many other parts of this trail are alive with mosquitos — so it may be wise to DEETify yourself once or twice during the hike.

The path leaves the marsh and divides about a half-mile from the trailhead — one branch heading west toward the river, the other southeast. They will meet again in about 0.3 miles, so take one branch going and the other on the return. In either case the path soon enters drier terrain and leads through forests and then back to the river. About 1.5

Marsh grasses in autumn

miles from trailhead, the view opens out onto a grassy field and Columbine Bay.

The bay is bordered by coniferous forests of fir, spruce and pine — the stand extending up the surrounding mountains. A hazy field of grass carpets the east shore, and accentuates the serene beauty of the scene. Past this point, Columbine Bay joins Grand Bay, and farther south Grand Bay enters Lake Granby. The East Shore Trail continues for more than 11 miles to the Arapaho Bay Ranger Station, with the last 5 miles of the trail outside of the park's boundary.

Hiking this trail in autumn brings additional pleasures. A few hard frosts solve the mosquito problem, and with fewer visitors there is more solitude. The marshy areas are mostly dry, and the grasses are in full-plumed glory with color nearer to gold than to tan, giving an impressionistic softness to the riverside scenery, but a hard-edged contrast to the mountains.

To Calypso Bay — Winter

Whether on snowshoes or skis, a winter excursion to Calypso Bay is a pleasant experience. Of course, the marsh grasses and forest groundcovers are now masked by snow, but in return there is a starkly beautiful study in black and white. The trees are black in the light of a sun now too

Snowshoeing along the Colorado River (photo by Susan Malitz)

weak to fire up any color; even the river flows black, its blackness accentuated by razored slashes of white reflections and shards of ice.

At one point, about one mile from the trailhead, the trail leads out of the forest to a sweeping view of the Colorado River, thirty paces or so off the path. Then the trail ascends, as it cuts its narrow way across a rather steep hillside, steep enough to pose an avalanche threat.

One can avoid this section of the trail by going down to the river before the climb begins. Close to the river's edge there is an alternate route, usually well marked by ski travel, that parallels the official path. Most will find the alternate route easier, safer, and more scenic. However, this route soon runs into a promontory of rock that juts out toward the river, ending exactly at its edge. Stepping stones in shallow water provide a way around it — but take care, the stones may be slippery, and unstable.

Past this obstacle, the treeless shore widens to as much as 300 feet from river to forest. Some may find this part of the hike a bit unvarying, but it does have an austere beauty that evokes a profound sense of solitude. The scene doesn't change for most of a mile; but when it does, assuming that you have taken the shoreline route, you find the way impeded by a jumble of boulders at the head of Columbine Bay — a likely place to turn back.

The trail from Shadow Mountain Lake to Columbine Bay is a hike for all seasons, and a special treat for those with a fondness for rivery scenery.

Shadow Mountain

Trailhead (1):	East Shore Trailhead, parking at Shadow Mountain Dam 3 miles south of the Grand Lake entrance station
Distance:	4.8 miles
Altitude gain:	1,530 feet
Elevation at destination:	9,920 feet

The hike to the top of Shadow Mountain is varied and highly scenic, and its location at the southwest corner of the Park enhances its appeal for those seeking solitude. The trail offers extraordinary lake scenery, unusual rock formations, comfortable walking in the shade of conifers, and superb views from the fire lookout station near the summit.

There are two approaches to the trail that leads up the mountain. One is via the town of Grand Lake: go east off U.S. 34, turn right at the post office, cross the bridge spanning the canal joining Grand Lake and Shadow Mountain Lake to road's end, park, and follow the trail along

Grand Lake from the fire lookout

Rock formations near the midway mark

the west shore of Shadow Mountain Lake about 1.5 miles to where the Shadow Mountain Trail branches off to the right. The other route begins at the southern tip of Shadow Mountain Dam: drive east off U.S. 34 to the Green Ridge Campground, park, walk across the spillway, walk north for about 1.5 miles along the west shore of Shadow Mountain Lake, and turn right onto the Shadow Mountain Trail. The second route is a bit shorter and may be a bit more scenic, but it's a toss-up.

Either starting point begins a walk along the eastern shore of Shadow Mountain Lake — slow-going since there is a photo opportunity every few steps. During the summer, the trail is mostly dry; where there is a bit of marshiness, feathery horsetails make a carpet of brightest green.

After about 1.5 miles from either starting point, a sign marks the side trail to the fire lookout 3.3 miles away. The path turns sharply to the southeast, and begins to snake its way up the mountain through forest of pine. The climb is mostly gradual and the path mostly uncluttered, but a few sections are steeper and rockier, particularly near the beginning and the end.

Midway along the ascent is an extraordinary boulder outcropping — the dark gray granite folded and fluted into soft forms that mock the rock. In the crevices tufts of greenish white flowered heuchera and emerald green moss further heighten the illusion of plush softness. This show is repeated again further along the trail, with a final, less dramatic encore near the end.

About a mile from the lookout tower, at the elbow of a switchback, a small stream emerges from the hillside. Its flow, partly directed along a hollow log, splashes onto a bed of moss studded with clumps of golden-flowered mimulus. From here it's only a crooked mile to the lookout; still, the forest is dense enough to permit only tantalizing, slivered views of the lakes.

Even at the base of the fire lookout the boulders and trees block the view. But climb a few flights of stairs to the upper deck and there you have it all: Grand Lake and Shadow Mountain Lake spread 1,500 feet below you, surrounded by mountains.

Those preferring a walk with less elevation gain can opt for a 3-mile shore tour from the town of Grand Lake to Shadow Mountain Dam (or the reverse) by arranging a two-car shuttle, or make it a two-way 6-mile stroll, or walk part way and then back from either starting point — none of these options will disappoint you.

Adams Falls

Trailhead (2):	East Inlet Trailhead in Grand Lake
Distance one way:	0.3 miles
Altitude gain:	80 feet
Elevation at destination:	8,470 feet

The trail to Adams Falls is the most popular walk in the Grand Lake region of the park — a short and easy stroll to a pleasant waterfall and some superb river scenery.

On U.S. 34 there is a small kiosk that serves as a tourist information center. Immediately to the south of the kiosk, a side road leaves the highway and heads east to the center of Grand Lake where it joins a road (left) to Adams Falls. Parking at the East Inlet trailhead is ample, and space is almost guaranteed, even though the walk to the falls is quite popular.

The gentle trail winds its way east through a pleasant coniferous forest. Bordering the trail in several places are some extraordinary outcroppings of gray-black rock. Deeply pleated and pillowy in form, they contradict the stuff they are made of.

The path leads to a rock ledge overlook, shear to the falls below. The falls are beautiful, but of modest size and most of the dramatic portion is hidden away. However, the upper cascade is in full view as it careens through a shallow canyon down to the brink of the falls.

Scrambling down to the river bank brings you quite close to the lower falls, but here too the surrounding rock blocks a clear view. The river quickly spreads out, and during the drier part of the season can be easily forded, providing that care is taken not to slip on the slick algae-coated rocks. Once on the other side, there is an unobstructed view of the lower falls, but there is no need to cross over in order to enjoy the superb river scenery.

The river can be followed downstream for half a mile or so. In some places pine and fir encroach upon the shore; in others, the shore is skirted with grasses of several species — some gracefully arching, others emphatically vertical. The scene may be at its best in autumn when frost burnishes the grasses to silky tan and brassy yellow, and furnishes them with an assortment of distinctive seed heads. Autumn also curbs the number of visitors, and the cooler temperature is perfect for hiking.

The hike described here is the initial section of the East Inlet Trail which continues past the waterfall. The scenery is pleasant, and about a half-mile from the falls the trail passes close enough to East Inlet to provide excellent river scenery. The first major feature is Lone Pine Lake, 5.5 miles from the trailhead.

Adams Falls

Lichen and moss-covered cliff beside Adams Falls

Onahu - Tonahutu - Green Mountain Trail

Trailhead (3,4):	Onahu Trailhead or Green Mountain Trailhead 3.3 miles north of the Grand Lake entrance
Distance (complete loop):	6.5 miles
Altitude gain:	820 feet (from 8,850 feet to 9,670 feet, and back)

The Onahu, Tonahutu, and Green Mountain trails conveniently intersect to form a circle route through a variety of pleasant terrain, including several sites of historical interest. The hike is easy, although there are a few steep sections of moderately short duration.

The hike can start at either the Green Mountain Trailhead or the Onahu Creek Trailhead. Those prefering to complete a hike with a downhill stretch, should start at the former. A willing chauffeur can leave the rest of the group at the Onahu Creek Trailhead, and drop the car off at the Green Mountain Trailhead — a saving of a 0.5 miles and a few dozen feet of elevation gain for which the driver is rewarded with a pleasant stroll through mixed forest of pine, spruce, fir, and some fine stands of aspen, although the sight and sound of highway traffic will be an unwelcomed companion throughout this short stretch.

Starting at the Onahu Creek Trailhead, an initial hilly ascent of about a mile through forest of aspen and pine, then pine, spruce and fir, brings you to a bridge that crosses Onahu Creek. Although not a raging torrent, the whitewater has action enough to counterpoint the moss-covered rocks and abundant flowers on the banks. At 2 miles from trailhead, a sign announces that Onahu Bridge, your next destination, is half a mile further on. The path leads away from the water through lodgepole forest, and then comes back to the creek to cross it. Here it joins the Timber Creek Trail which you follow to the right (south).

A few hundred feet brings you to a junction of trails and a confusion of signs — continue in the same direction, heading south toward Big Meadows. Now the trail ascends more steeply, crossing a gray-black jumble of granite boulders — this is an edge moraine, detritus scooped up and deposited at the sides of a glacier. Then it's back to the forest.

Lodgepole pine

Big Meadows

One of Sam Stone's cabins

This time it's pure lodgepole pine in such an extraordinary dense pack that visibility is cut to a couple of dozen feet.

Continuing south, 1.3 miles from its intersection with the Onahu Trail, the Timber Creek Trail is met by the Tonahutu Trail entering from the east, and a sign announces that Bear Lake is 13.5 miles away — a bit more than twice the distance of this hike. Ignoring the temptation, continue south to Big Meadows on what is now the Tonahutu Trail. And big it is — a sea of wild flowers and grasses rimmed by hills. You get to view it from the shade of the forest, and it's a picture worth taking.

About midway along the meadows stand two trailside cabins, former property of Sam Stone. He built them around 1900, one to house himself, the other his livestock. He earned his livelihood by selling hay harvested from the meadow at his doorstep. But then he met a woman who convinced him that gold was to be found in what is now the southern part of the park. So Sam abandoned his homestead and went in pursuit of the lady and the precious metal — and never was heard from again.

At the south end of the meadow the Green Mountain Trail crosses the Tonahutu Trail. You turn right onto the Green Mountain Trail and follow it west back to the trailhead for an easy 1.8 miles through a pleasant evergreen forest.

Bibliography

GEOLOGY
Richmond, Gerald M., *Raising the Roof of the Rockies*, Estes Park, CO: Rocky Mountain Nature Association, 1974.

FLORA AND FAUNA
Armstrong, David M., *Rocky Mountain Mammals*, Estes Park, CO: Rocky Mountain Nature Association, 1975.
Craighead, John J., Craighead, Frank C., and Davis, Ray J., *Rocky Mountain Wildflowers*, Boston, MA: Houghton Mifflin Company, 1963.
Dannen, Donna, and Dannen, Kent, *Rocky Mountain Wildflowers*, Estes Park, CO: Tundra Publications, 1987.
Torbit, Stephan C., *Large Mammals of the Central Rockies*, Monte Vista, CO: Bennet Creek Publications, 1987.
Udvardi, Miklos D., *Audubon Society Field Guide to North American Birds, Western Region*, New York, NY: Knopf, 1977.
Watts, Tom, *Rocky Mountain Tree Finder*, Berkeley, CA: Nature Guide, 1972.
Weber, William A., *Rocky Mountain Flora*, 5 th ed., Boulder, CO: Colorado Associated University Press, 1976.

GENERAL
Mills, Enos A., *The Spell of the Rockies*, Lincoln, NE: University of Nebraska Press, 1987.
Trimble, Stephan, *Longs Peak*, Estes Park, CO: Rocky Mountain Nature Association, 1984.
Willard, Beatrice Elizabeth and Foster, Susan Quimby, *A Roadside Guide to Rocky Mountain National Park*, Boulder, CO: Johnson Books, 1990.

HIKING AND CAMPING
Dannen, Donna,and Dannen, Kent, *Rocky Mountain National Park Hiking Trails*, 6th ed., Chester, CT: Globe Piquot Press, 1985.
Dannen, Donna, and Dannen, Kent, *Short Hikes in Rocky Mountain National Park*, Estes Park, CO: Tundra Publications, 1986.
Erik Nilsson, *Rocky Mountain National Park Trail Guide*, World Publication, 1978.

HISTORY
Buchholtz, Curt W., *Rocky Mountain National Park: a History*, Boulder CO: Colorado Associated University Press, 1983.

Index

This index is limited to proper place names. Each entry which is a destination of a hike featured in the text is in **bold** type. The numbers in parenthesese rank the comparative difficulty of the hike and were determined by equating 1,000 feet of elevation gain with a walk of two miles, and then adding this to the number of miles required for the round trip. For example, Mills Lake is 2.5 miles from the Glacier Gorge Junction Trailhead and the hike requires a climb of 700 feet. The rating under this sytem is:

$$(0.002 \times \text{elevation gain}) + \text{distance round trip} = \text{rating}$$
$$(0.002 \times 700) + 5.0 = 6.4$$

As a rule of thumb, we regard a hike as easy if the rating is less than 6; moderate if between 6 and 10; and difficult if greater than 10. My thanks to Dick Holley for suggesting this formula; it meshes nicely with intuitive estimates of the effort required.